GW00492559

501

MUST-VISIT DESTINATIONS
TRAVEL JOURNAL

Bounty
Books

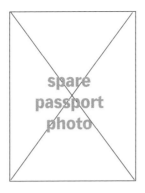

spare
passport
photo

This journal belongs to

NAME:

ADDRESS:

TELEPHONE:

EMAIL:

Please return if found.

Thank you.

A footbridge leads to the castle at Matsumoto, Japan

Weights and measures

Metric measurements

LENGTH

1 millimetre (mm)		= 0.0394 in
1 centimetre (cm)	= 10 mm	= 0.3937 in
1 metre (m)	= 100 cm	= 1.0936 yd
1 kilometre (km)	= 1,000 m	= 0.6214 mile

AREA

1 sq cm (cm^2)	= 100 mm^2	= 0.155 in^2
1 sq metre (m^2)	= 10, 000 cm^2	= 1.196 yd^2
1 sq km (km^2)	= 100 hectares	= 0.3861 mile^2

WEIGHT

1 milligram (mg)		= 0.0154 grain
1 gram (g)	= 1,000 mg	= 0.0353 oz
1 kilogram (kg)	= 1,000 g	= 2.2046 lb
1 tonne (t)	= 1,000 kg	= 0.9842 ton

VOLUME

1 cu cm (cm^3)		= 0.061 in^3
1 cu decimetre (dm^3)	= 1,000 cm^3	= 0.0353 ft^3
1 cu metre (m^3)	= 1,000 dm^3	= 1.308 yd^3
1 litre (l)	= 1 dm^3	= 1.76 pt
		= 2.113 US pt
1 hectolitre (hl)	= 100 l	= 21.997 gal
		= 26.417 US gal

Imperial measurements

LENGTH

1 inch (in)		= 2.54 cm
1 foot (ft)	= 12 in	= 0.3048 m
1 yard (yd)	= 3 ft	= 0.9144 m
1 mile	= 1,760 yd	= 1.6093 km
1 nautical mile	= 2,025.4 yd	= 1.852 km

AREA

1 sq inch (in^2)		= 6.4516 cm^2
1 sq foot (ft^2)	= 144 in^2	= 0.0929 m^2
1 sq yard (yd^2)	= 9 ft^2	= 0.8361 m^2
1 acre	= 4,840 yd^2	= 4,046.9 m^2
1 sq mile (mile^2)	= 640 acres	= 2.59 km^2

WEIGHT

1 ounce (oz)	= 437.5 grains	= 28.35 g
1 pound (lb)	= 16 oz	= 0.4536 kg
1 stone	= 14 lb	= 6.3503 kg
1 hundredweight (cwt)	= 112 lb	= 50.802 kg
1 ton	= 20 cwt	= 1.016 t

VOLUME

1 cu inch (in^3)		= 16.387 cm^3
1 cu foot (ft^3)	= 1,728 in^3	= 0.0283 m^3
1 cu yard (yd^3)	= 27 ft^3	= 0.7646 m^3
1 fluid ounce (fl oz)		= 28.413 ml
1 pint (pt)	= 20 fl oz	= 0.5683 l
1 gallon (gal)	= 8 pt	= 4.546 l

KILOMETRES	km or miles	MILES
1.61	1	0.62
3.22	2	1.24
4.83	3	1.86
6.44	4	2.48
8.05	5	3.11
9.66	6	3.73
11.26	7	4.35
12.87	8	4.97
14.48	9	5.59
16.09	10	6.21
32.19	20	12.43
48.28	30	16.64
64.37	40	24.85
80.47	50	31.07
96.56	60	37.28
112.65	70	43.50
128.75	80	49.71
144.84	90	55.93
160.93	100	62.14

CONVERSIONS

KILOGRAMS	kg or lb	POUNDS
0.45	1	2.20
0.91	2	4.41
1.36	3	6.61
1.81	4	8.82
2.27	5	11.02
2.72	6	13.29
3.17	7	15.43
3.63	8	17.64
4.08	9	19.84
4.54	10	22.05
9.07	20	44.09
13.61	30	66.14
18.14	40	88.18
22.68	50	110.23
27.22	60	132.28
31.75	70	154.32
36.29	80	176.37
40.82	90	198.42
45.36	100	220.46

Temperature

Celsius = 5/9 (fahrenheit − 32)

Fahrenheit = 9/5 celsius + 32

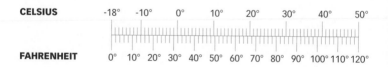

Clothing and shoes

Women's clothes

UK	USA	EUROPE
8	6	36
10	8	38
12	10	40
14	12	42
16	14	44
18	16	46/48
20	18	50
22	20	52

Men's shirts

UK	USA	EUROPE
14	14	36
$14\frac{1}{2}$	$14\frac{1}{2}$	37
15	15	38
$15\frac{1}{2}$	$15\frac{1}{2}$	39
16	16	40
16	$16\frac{1}{2}$	41
$16\frac{1}{2}$	17	42

Men's suits

UK	USA	EUROPE
34	34	44
36	36	46
38	38	48
40	40	50
42	42	52
44	44	54

Women's shoes

UK	USA	EUROPE
3	$4\frac{1}{2}$	35
4	$5\frac{1}{2}$	37
5	$6\frac{1}{2}$	38
6	$7\frac{1}{2}$	39
7	$8\frac{1}{2}$	40
8	$9\frac{1}{2}$	41

Men's shoes

UK	USA	EUROPE
6	7-$7\frac{1}{2}$	40
7	8	41
8	9	42
9	10	43
10	11	44
11	12	45

WORLD TIME ZONES

10 Hours behind or ahead of GMT

Zones using GMT

Zones behind GMT

International boundaries

Zones ahead of GMT

WORLD TIME ZONES

Half-hour zones	Actual solar time when time at Greenwich is 12.00 (noon)
Time zone boundaries	
International date line	Note: Some of the above time zones are affected by daylight saving time in countries where it is adopted.

Cartography © Philip's

Average annual precipitation

3,000 mm
2,000 mm
1,000 mm
500 mm
250 mm

Cartography © Philip's

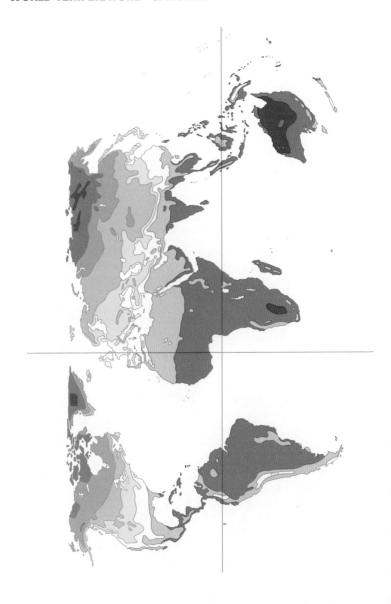

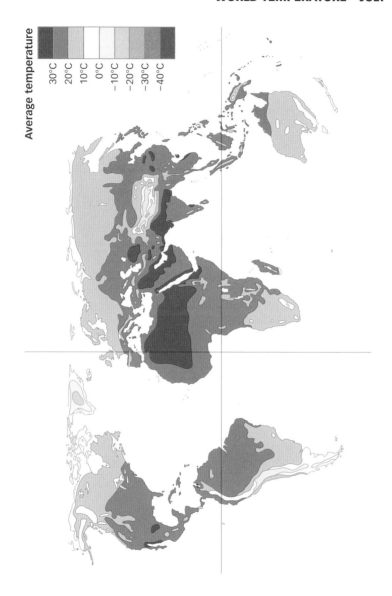

Average temperature

30°C 20°C 10°C 0°C -10°C -20°C -30°C -40°C

Cartography © Philip's

WORLD WEATHER GUIDE

		J	**F**	**M**	**A**	**M**	**J**	**J**	**A**	**S**	**O**	**N**	**D**
Amsterdam, Netherlands													
Temp °C	max	4	5	10	13	18	21	22	22	19	14	9	5
	min	−1	−1	1	4	8	11	13	13	10	7	3	1
Temp °F	max	40	42	49	56	64	70	72	71	67	57	48	42
	min	31	31	34	40	46	51	55	55	50	44	38	33
Precipitation (mm)		68	53	44	49	52	58	77	87	72	72	70	64
Humidity %	am	90	90	86	79	75	75	79	82	86	90	92	91
	pm	82	76	65	61	59	59	64	65	67	72	81	85
Athens, Greece													
Temp °C	max	13	14	16	20	25	30	33	33	29	24	19	15
	min	6	7	8	11	16	20	23	23	19	15	12	8
Temp °F	max	55	57	60	68	77	86	92	92	84	75	66	58
	min	44	44	46	52	61	68	73	73	67	60	53	47
Precipitation (mm)		62	37	37	23	23	14	6	7	15	51	56	71
Humidity %	am	77	74	71	65	60	50	47	48	58	70	78	78
	pm	62	57	54	48	47	39	34	34	42	52	61	63
Auckland, New Zealand													
Temp °C	max	23	23	22	19	17	14	13	14	16	17	19	21
	min	16	16	15	13	11	9	8	8	8	11	12	14
Temp °F	max	73	73	71	67	62	58	56	58	60	63	66	70
	min	60	60	59	56	51	48	46	46	49	52	54	57
Precipitation (mm)		79	94	81	97	127	137	145	117	102	102	89	79
Humidity %	am	71	72	74	78	80	83	84	80	76	74	71	70
	pm	62	61	65	69	70	73	74	70	68	66	64	64
Bangkok, Thailand													
Temp °C	max	32	33	34	35	34	33	32	32	32	31	31	31
	min	20	22	24	25	25	24	24	24	24	24	22	20
Temp °F	max	89	91	93	95	93	91	90	90	90	88	88	87
	min	68	72	75	77	77	76	76	76	76	75	72	68
Precipitation (mm)		8	20	36	58	198	160	160	175	305	206	66	5
Humidity %	am	91	92	92	90	91	90	91	92	94	93	92	91
	pm	53	55	56	58	64	67	66	66	70	70	65	56
Berlin, Germany													
Temp °C	max	2	3	8	13	19	22	24	23	20	13	7	3
	min	−3	−3	0	4	8	12	14	13	10	6	2	−1
Temp °F	max	35	37	46	56	66	72	75	74	68	56	45	38
	min	26	26	32	39	47	53	57	56	50	42	36	29
Precipitation (mm)		46	40	33	42	49	65	73	69	48	49	46	43
Humidity %	am	89	89	88	84	80	80	84	88	92	93	92	91
	pm	82	78	67	60	57	58	61	61	65	73	83	86

		J	F	M	A	M	J	J	A	S	O	N	D
Mumbai (Bombay), India													
Temp °C	max	28	28	30	32	33	32	29	29	29	32	32	31
	min	12	12	17	20	23	21	22	22	22	21	18	13
Temp °F	max	83	83	86	89	91	89	85	85	85	89	89	87
	min	67	67	72	76	80	79	77	77	77	76	73	69
Precipitation (mm)		2.5	2.5	2.5	0	18	485	617	340	264	64	13	2.5
Humidity %	am	70	71	73	75	74	79	83	83	85	81	73	70
	pm	61	62	65	67	68	77	83	81	78	71	64	62
Brussels, Belgium													
Temp °C	max	4	7	10	14	18	22	23	22	21	15	9	6
	min	−1	0	2	5	8	11	12	12	11	7	3	0
Temp °F	max	40	44	51	58	65	72	73	72	69	60	48	42
	min	30	32	36	41	46	52	54	54	51	45	38	32
Precipitation (mm)		66	61	53	60	55	76	95	80	63	83	75	88
Humidity %	am	92	92	91	91	90	87	91	93	94	93	93	92
	pm	86	81	74	71	65	65	68	69	69	77	85	86
Buenos Aires, Argentina													
Temp °C	max	29	28	26	22	18	14	14	16	18	21	24	28
	min	17	17	16	12	8	5	6	6	8	10	13	16
Temp °F	max	85	83	79	72	64	57	57	60	64	69	76	82
	min	63	63	60	53	47	41	42	42	46	50	56	61
Precipitation (mm)		79	71	109	89	76	61	56	61	79	86	84	99
Humidity %	am	81	83	87	88	90	91	92	90	86	83	79	79
	pm	61	63	69	71	74	78	79	74	68	65	60	62
Cairo, Egypt													
Temp °C	max	18	21	24	28	33	35	36	35	32	30	26	20
	min	8	9	11	14	17	20	21	22	20	18	14	10
Temp °F	max	65	69	75	83	91	95	6	95	90	86	78	68
	min	47	48	52	57	63	68	70	71	68	65	56	50
Precipitation (mm)		5	5	5	3	3	0	0	0	0	0	3	5
Humidity %	am	69	64	63	55	50	55	65	69	68	67	68	70
	pm	40	33	27	21	18	20	24	28	31	31	38	41
Kolkata (Calcutta), India													
Temp °C	max	27	29	34	36	36	33	32	32	32	32	29	26
	min	13	15	21	24	25	26	26	26	26	24	18	13
Temp °F	max	80	84	93	97	97	92	89	89	89	89	84	79
	min	55	59	69	75	77	79	79	76	78	74	64	55
Precipitation (mm)		10	31	36	43	140	297	325	328	252	114	20	5
Humidity %	am	85	82	79	76	77	82	86	88	86	85	79	80
	pm	52	45	46	56	62	75	80	82	81	72	63	55

WORLD WEATHER GUIDE

		J	**F**	**M**	**A**	**M**	**J**	**J**	**A**	**S**	**O**	**N**	**D**

Colombo, Sri Lanka

		J	F	M	A	M	J	J	A	S	O	N	D
Temp °C	max	30	31	31	31	31	29	29	29	29	29	29	29
	min	22	22	23	24	26	25	25	25	25	24	23	22
Temp °F	max	86	87	87	87	87	85	85	85	85	85	85	85
	min	72	72	74	76	78	77	77	77	77	75	73	72
Precipitation (mm)		89	69	147	231	371	224	135	109	160	348	315	147
Humidity %	am	73	71	71	74	78	80	79	78	76	77	77	74
	pm	67	66	66	70	76	78	77	76	75	76	75	69

Copenhagen, Denmark

		J	F	M	A	M	J	J	A	S	O	N	D
Temp °C	max	2	2	5	10	16	19	22	21	18	12	7	4
	min	−2	−3	−1	3	8	11	14	14	11	7	3	1
Temp °F	max	36	36	41	51	61	67	71	70	64	54	45	40
	min	28	28	31	38	46	52	57	56	51	44	38	34
Precipitation (mm)		49	39	32	38	43	47	71	66	62	59	48	49
Humidity %	am	88	86	85	79	70	70	74	78	83	86	88	89
	pm	85	83	78	68	59	60	62	64	69	76	83	87

Delhi, India

		J	F	M	A	M	J	J	A	S	O	N	D
Temp °C	max	21	24	31	36	41	39	36	34	34	31	29	23
	min	7	9	14	20	26	28	27	26	24	18	11	8
Temp °F	max	70	75	87	97	105	102	96	93	93	93	84	73
	min	44	49	58	68	79	83	81	79	75	65	52	46
Precipitation (mm)		23	18	13	8	13	74	180	173	117	10	3	10
Humidity %	am	72	67	49	35	35	53	75	80	72	56	51	69
	pm	41	35	23	19	20	36	59	64	51	32	31	42

Harare, Zimbabwe

		J	F	M	A	M	J	J	A	S	O	N	D
Temp °C	max	26	26	26	26	23	21	21	23	26	28	27	26
	min	16	16	14	13	9	7	7	8	12	14	16	16
Temp °F	max	78	78	78	78	74	70	70	74	79	83	81	79
	min	60	60	58	55	49	44	44	47	53	58	60	60
Precipitation (mm)		196	178	117	28	13	3	0	3	5	29	97	163
Humidity %	am	74	77	75	68	60	58	56	50	43	43	56	67
	pm	57	53	52	44	37	36	33	28	26	26	43	57

Hong Kong

		J	F	M	A	M	J	J	A	S	O	N	D
Temp °C	max	18	17	19	24	28	29	31	31	29	27	23	20
	min	13	13	16	19	23	26	26	26	25	23	18	15
Temp °F	max	64	63	67	75	82	85	87	87	85	81	74	68
	min	56	55	60	67	74	78	78	78	77	73	65	59
Precipitation (mm)		33	46	74	137	292	394	381	367	257	114	43	31
Humidity %	am	77	82	84	87	87	86	87	87	83	75	73	74
	pm	66	73	74	77	78	77	77	77	72	63	60	63

		J	F	M	A	M	J	J	A	S	O	N	D
Istanbul, Turkey													
Temp °C	max	8	9	11	16	21	25	28	28	24	20	15	11
	min	3	2	3	7	12	16	18	19	16	13	9	5
Temp °F	max	46	47	51	60	69	77	82	82	76	68	59	51
	min	37	36	38	45	53	60	65	66	61	55	48	41
Precipitation (mm)		109	92	72	46	38	34	34	30	58	81	103	119
Humidity %	am	82	82	81	81	82	79	79	79	81	83	82	82
	pm	75	72	67	62	61	58	56	55	59	64	71	74
Jakarta, Indonesia													
Temp °C	max	29	9	30	31	31	31	31	31	31	31	30	29
	min	23	23	23	24	24	23	23	23	23	23	23	23
Temp °F	max	84	84	86	87	87	87	87	87	87	87	86	85
	min	74	74	74	75	75	74	73	73	74	74	74	75
Precipitation (mm)		300	300	211	147	114	97	64	43	66	112	142	203
Humidity %	am	95	95	94	94	94	93	92	90	90	90	92	92
	pm	75	75	73	71	69	67	64	61	62	64	68	71
Jerusalem, Israel													
Temp °C	max	13	13	18	23	27	29	31	31	29	27	21	15
	min	5	6	8	10	14	16	17	18	17	15	12	7
Temp °F	max	55	56	65	73	81	85	87	87	85	81	70	59
	min	41	42	46	50	57	60	63	64	62	59	53	45
Precipitation (mm)		132	132	64	28	3	0	0	0	0	13	71	86
Humidity %	am	77	74	61	56	47	48	52	58	61	60	65	73
	pm	66	58	57	42	33	32	35	36	36	36	50	60
Johannesburg, South Africa													
Temp °C	max	26	25	24	22	19	17	17	20	23	25	25	26
	min	14	14	13	10	6	4	4	6	9	12	13	14
Temp °F	max	78	77	75	72	66	62	63	68	73	77	77	78
	min	58	58	55	50	43	39	39	43	48	53	55	57
Precipitation (mm)		114	109	89	38	25	8	8	8	23	56	107	125
Humidity %	am	75	78	79	74	70	70	69	64	59	64	67	70
	pm	50	53	50	44	36	33	32	29	30	37	45	47
Kathmandu, Nepal													
Temp °C	max	18	19	25	28	30	29	29	28	28	27	23	19
	min	2	4	7	12	16	19	20	20	19	30	7	3
Temp °F	max	65	67	77	83	86	85	84	83	83	80	74	67
	min	35	39	45	53	61	67	68	68	66	56	45	37
Precipitation (mm)		15	41	23	58	122	246	378	345	155	38	8	3
Humidity %	am	89	90	73	68	72	79	86	87	86	88	90	89
	pm	70	68	53	54	61	72	82	84	83	81	78	73

WORLD WEATHER GUIDE

		J	F	M	A	M	J	J	A	S	O	N	D
Kuala Lumpur, Malaysia													
Temp °C	max	32	33	33	33	33	33	32	32	32	32	32	32
	min	22	22	23	23	23	22	23	23	23	23	23	22
Temp °F	max	90	92	92	92	92	92	90	90	90	89	89	89
	min	72	72	73	73	73	72	73	73	73	73	73	72
Precipitation (mm)		158	201	259	292	224	130	99	163	218	249	259	191
Humidity %	am	97	97	97	97	97	96	95	96	96	96	97	97
	pm	60	60	58	63	66	63	63	62	64	65	66	61
Lima, Peru													
Temp °C	max	28	28	28	27	23	20	19	19	20	22	23	26
	min	19	19	19	17	16	14	14	13	14	14	16	17
Temp °F	max	83	83	83	80	74	68	67	66	68	71	74	78
	min	66	66	66	63	60	58	57	56	57	58	63	62
Precipitation (mm)		3	0	0	0	5	5	8	8	8	3	3	0
Humidity %	am	93	92	92	93	95	95	94	95	94	94	93	93
	pm	69	66	64	66	76	80	77	78	76	72	71	70
Lisbon, Portugal													
Temp °C	max	14	15	17	20	21	25	27	28	26	22	17	15
	min	8	8	10	12	13	15	17	17	17	14	11	9
Temp °F	max	57	59	63	67	71	77	81	82	79	72	63	58
	min	46	47	50	53	55	60	63	63	62	58	52	47
Precipitation (mm)		111	76	109	54	44	16	3	4	33	62	93	103
Humidity %	am	85	80	78	69	68	65	62	64	70	75	81	84
	pm	71	64	64	56	57	54	48	49	54	59	68	72
London, England													
Temp °C	max	6	7	10	13	17	20	22	21	19	14	10	7
	min	2	2	3	6	8	12	14	13	11	8	5	4
Temp °F	max	43	44	50	56	62	69	71	71	65	58	50	45
	min	36	36	38	42	47	53	56	56	52	46	42	38
Precipitation (mm)		54	40	37	37	46	45	57	59	49	57	64	48
Humidity %	am	86	85	81	71	70	70	71	76	80	85	85	87
	pm	77	72	64	56	57	58	59	62	65	70	78	81
Madrid, Spain													
Temp °C	max	9	11	15	18	21	27	31	30	25	19	13	9
	min	2	2	5	7	10	15	17	17	14	10	5	2
Temp °F	max	47	52	59	65	70	80	87	85	77	65	55	48
	min	35	36	41	45	50	58	63	63	57	49	42	36
Precipitation (mm)		39	34	43	48	47	27	11	15	32	53	47	48
Humidity %	am	86	83	80	74	72	66	58	62	72	81	84	86
	pm	71	62	56	49	49	41	33	35	46	58	65	70

		J	F	M	A	M	J	J	A	S	O	N	D

Manila, Philippines

Temp °C	max	30	31	33	34	34	33	31	31	31	31	31	30
	min	21	21	22	23	24	24	24	24	24	23	22	21
Temp °F	max	86	88	91	93	93	91	88	87	88	88	88	86
	min	69	69	71	73	75	75	75	75	75	74	73	70
Precipitation (mm)		23	13	18	33	130	254	432	422	356	193	145	66
Humidity %	am	89	88	85	85	88	91	91	92	93	92	91	90
	pm	63	59	55	55	61	68	74	73	73	71	69	67

Melbourne, Australia

Temp °C	max	26	26	24	20	17	14	13	15	17	19	22	24
	min	14	14	13	11	8	7	6	6	8	9	11	12
Temp °F	max	78	78	75	68	62	57	56	59	63	67	71	75
	min	57	57	55	51	47	44	42	43	46	48	51	54
Precipitation (mm)		48	46	56	58	53	53	48	48	58	66	58	58
Humidity %	am	58	62	64	72	79	83	82	76	68	61	60	59
	pm	48	50	51	56	62	67	65	60	55	52	52	51

Mexico City, Mexico

Temp °C	max	19	21	24	25	26	24	23	23	23	21	20	19
	min	6	6	8	11	12	13	12	12	12	10	8	6
Temp °F	max	66	69	75	77	78	76	73	73	73	70	68	66
	min	42	43	47	51	54	55	53	53	53	50	46	43
Precipitation (mm)		13	5	10	20	53	119	170	152	130	51	18	8
Humidity %	am	79	72	68	66	69	82	84	85	86	83	82	81
	pm	34	28	26	29	29	48	50	50	54	47	41	37

Miami, USA

Temp °C	max	23	24	26	27	29	30	31	31	31	28	26	24
	min	16	16	18	19	22	23	24	24	24	22	19	17
Temp °F	max	74	75	78	80	84	86	88	88	88	83	78	76
	min	61	61	64	67	71	74	76	76	76	72	66	62
Precipitation (mm)		71	53	64	81	173	178	155	160	203	234	71	51
Humidity %	am	81	82	77	73	75	75	75	76	79	80	77	82
	pm	66	63	62	64	67	69	68	68	70	69	64	65

Moscow, Russia

Temp °C	max	−9	−6	0	10	19	21	23	22	16	9	2	−5
	min	−16	−14	−8	1	8	11	13	12	7	3	−3	−10
Temp °F	max	15	22	32	50	66	70	73	72	61	48	35	24
	min	3	8	18	34	46	51	55	53	45	37	26	15
Precipitation (mm)		39	38	36	37	53	58	88	71	58	45	47	54
Humidity %	am	82	82	82	73	58	62	68	74	78	81	87	85
	pm	77	66	64	54	43	47	54	55	59	67	79	83

WORLD WEATHER GUIDE

Nairobi, Kenya

		J	F	M	A	M	J	J	A	S	O	N	D
Temp °C	max	25	26	25	24	22	21	21	21	24	24	23	23
	min	12	13	14	14	13	12	11	11	11	13	13	13
Temp °F	max	77	79	77	75	72	70	70	70	75	76	74	74
	min	54	55	57	57	56	53	52	52	52	55	56	55
Precipitation (mm)		38	64	125	211	158	46	15	23	31	53	109	86
Humidity %	am	74	74	81	88	88	89	86	86	82	82	86	81
	pm	44	40	45	56	62	60	58	56	45	43	53	53

Nassau, Bahamas

		J	F	M	A	M	J	J	A	S	O	N	D
Temp °C	max	25	25	26	27	29	31	31	32	31	59	27	26
	min	18	18	19	21	22	23	24	24	24	23	21	19
Temp °F	max	77	77	79	81	84	87	87	89	88	85	81	79
	min	65	64	66	69	71	74	75	75	75	73	70	67
Precipitation (mm)		36	38	36	64	117	163	147	135	165	165	71	33
Humidity %	am	84	82	81	79	79	81	80	82	84	83	83	84
	pm	64	62	64	65	65	68	69	70	73	71	68	66

New York, USA

		J	F	M	A	M	J	J	A	S	O	N	D
Temp °C	max	3	3	7	14	20	25	28	27	26	21	11	5
	min	-4	-4	-1	6	12	16	19	19	16	9	3	-2
Temp °F	max	37	37	45	57	68	77	82	80	79	69	51	41
	min	24	24	30	42	53	60	66	66	60	49	37	29
Precipitation (mm)		94	97	91	81	81	84	107	109	86	89	76	91
Humidity %	am	72	70	70	68	70	74	77	79	79	76	75	73
	pm	60	58	55	53	54	58	58	60	61	57	60	61

Oslo, Norway

		J	F	M	A	M	J	J	A	S	O	N	D
Temp °C	max	-2	-1	4	10	16	20	22	21	16	9	3	0
	min	-7	-7	-4	1	6	10	13	12	8	3	-1	-4
Temp °F	max	28	30	39	50	61	68	72	70	60	48	38	32
	min	19	19	25	34	43	50	55	53	46	38	31	25
Precipitation (mm)		49	35	26	43	44	70	82	95	81	74	68	63
Humidity %	am	86	82	80	75	68	69	74	79	85	88	88	87
	pm	82	74	64	57	52	55	59	61	66	72	83	85

Ottawa, Canada

		J	F	M	A	M	J	J	A	S	O	N	D
Temp °C	max	-6	-6	1	11	19	24	27	25	20	12	4	-4
	min	-16	-16	-9	-1	7	12	14	13	9	3	-3	-13
Temp °F	max	21	21	33	51	66	76	82	77	68	54	39	24
	min	3	3	16	31	44	54	58	55	48	37	26	9
Precipitation (mm)		74	56	71	69	64	89	86	66	81	74	76	66
Humidity %	am	83	88	84	76	77	80	80	84	90	86	84	83
	pm	76	73	66	58	55	56	53	54	59	63	68	75

		J	F	M	A	M	J	J	A	S	O	N	D
Papeete, French Polynesia													
Temp °C	max	32	32	32	32	31	30	30	30	30	31	31	31
	min	22	22	22	22	21	21	20	20	21	21	22	22
Temp °F	max	89	89	89	89	87	86	86	86	86	87	88	88
	min	72	72	72	72	70	69	68	68	69	70	71	72
Precipitation (mm)		252	244	429	142	102	76	53	43	53	89	150	249
Humidity %	am	82	82	84	85	84	85	83	83	81	79	80	81
	pm	77	77	78	78	78	79	77	78	76	76	77	78
Paris, France													
Temp °C	max	6	7	12	16	20	23	25	24	21	16	10	7
	min	1	1	4	6	10	13	15	14	12	8	5	2
Temp °F	max	43	45	54	60	68	73	76	75	70	60	50	44
	min	34	34	39	43	49	55	58	58	53	46	40	36
Precipitation (mm)		56	46	35	42	57	54	59	64	55	50	51	50
Humidity %	am	88	87	85	82	83	83	83	87	90	91	91	90
	pm	80	73	63	54	55	58	57	61	65	71	79	82
Prague, Czech Republic													
Temp °C	max	0	1	7	12	18	21	23	22	18	12	5	1
	min	−5	−4	−1	3	8	11	13	13	9	5	1	−3
Temp °F	max	31	34	44	54	64	70	73	72	65	53	42	34
	min	23	24	30	38	46	52	55	55	49	41	33	27
Precipitation (mm)		18	18	18	27	48	54	68	55	31	33	20	21
Humidity %	am	84	83	82	77	75	74	77	81	84	87	87	87
	pm	73	67	55	47	45	46	49	48	51	60	73	78
Rio de Janeiro, Brazil													
Temp °C	max	29	29	28	27	25	24	24	24	24	25	26	28
	min	23	23	22	21	19	18	17	18	18	19	20	22
Temp °F	max	84	85	83	80	77	76	75	76	75	77	79	82
	min	73	73	72	69	66	64	63	64	65	66	68	71
Precipitation (mm)		125	122	130	107	79	53	41	43	66	79	104	137
Humidity %	am	82	84	87	87	87	87	86	84	84	83	82	82
	pm	70	71	74	73	70	69	68	66	72	72	72	72
Rome, Italy													
Temp °C	max	11	13	15	19	23	28	30	30	26	22	16	13
	min	5	5	7	10	13	17	20	20	17	13	9	6
Temp °F	max	52	55	59	66	74	82	87	86	79	71	61	55
	min	40	42	45	50	56	63	67	67	62	55	49	14
Precipitation (mm)		71	62	57	51	46	37	15	21	63	99	129	93
Humidity %	am	85	86	83	83	77	74	70	73	83	86	87	85
	pm	68	64	56	54	54	48	42	43	50	59	66	70

WORLD WEATHER GUIDE

		J	F	M	A	M	J	J	A	S	O	N	D
San Francisco, USA													
Temp °C	max	13	15	16	17	17	19	18	18	21	20	17	14
	min	7	8	9	9	11	11	12	12	13	12	11	8
Temp °F	max	55	59	61	62	63	66	65	65	69	68	63	57
	min	45	47	48	49	51	52	53	53	55	54	51	47
Precipitation (mm)		119	97	79	38	18	3	0	0	8	25	64	112
Humidity %	am	85	84	83	83	85	88	91	92	88	85	83	83
	pm	69	66	61	61	62	64	69	70	63	58	60	68
Stockholm, Sweden													
Temp °C	max	−1	−1	3	8	14	19	22	20	15	9	5	2
	min	−5	−5	−4	1	6	11	14	13	9	5	1	−2
Temp °F	max	30	30	37	47	58	67	71	68	60	49	40	35
	min	22	22	26	34	43	51	57	56	49	41	34	29
Precipitation (mm)		43	30	25	31	34	45	61	76	60	48	53	48
Humidity %	am	85	83	82	76	66	68	74	81	87	88	89	88
	pm	83	77	68	60	53	55	59	64	69	76	85	86
Sydney, Australia													
Temp °C	max	26	26	24	22	19	16	16	17	19	22	23	25
	min	18	18	17	14	11	9	8	9	11	13	16	17
Temp °F	max	78	78	76	71	66	61	60	63	67	71	74	77
	min	65	65	63	58	52	48	46	48	51	56	60	63
Precipitation (mm)		89	102	127	135	127	117	117	76	74	71	74	74
Humidity %	am	68	71	73	76	77	77	76	72	67	65	65	66
	pm	64	65	65	64	63	62	60	56	55	57	60	62
Tehran, Iran													
Temp °C	max	7	10	15	22	28	34	37	36	32	24	17	11
	min	−3	0	4	9	14	19	22	22	18	12	6	1
Temp °F	max	45	50	59	71	82	93	99	97	90	76	63	51
	min	27	32	39	49	58	66	72	71	64	53	43	33
Precipitation (mm)		46	38	46	36	13	3	3	3	3	8	20	31
Humidity %	am	77	73	61	54	55	50	51	47	49	53	63	76
	pm	75	59	39	40	47	49	41	46	49	54	66	75
Tokyo, Japan													
Temp °C	max	8	9	12	17	22	24	28	30	26	21	16	11
	min	−2	−1	2	8	12	17	21	22	19	13	6	1
Temp °F	max	47	48	54	63	71	76	83	86	79	69	60	52
	min	29	31	36	46	54	63	70	72	66	55	46	33
Precipitation (mm)		48	74	107	135	147	165	142	152	234	208	97	56
Humidity %	am	73	71	75	81	85	89	91	92	91	88	83	77
	pm	48	48	53	59	62	68	69	66	68	64	58	51

		J	F	M	A	M	J	J	A	S	O	N	D
Vancouver, Canada													
Temp °C	max	5	7	10	14	18	21	23	23	18	14	9	6
	min	0	1	3	4	8	11	12	12	9	7	4	2
Temp °F	max	41	44	50	58	64	69	74	73	65	57	48	43
	min	32	34	37	40	46	52	54	54	49	44	39	35
Precipitation (mm)		218	147	127	84	71	64	31	43	91	147	211	224
Humidity %	am	93	91	91	89	88	87	89	90	92	92	91	91
	pm	85	78	70	67	63	65	62	62	72	80	84	88
Vienna, Austria													
Temp °C	max	1	3	8	15	19	23	25	24	20	14	7	3
	min	−4	−3	−1	6	10	14	15	15	11	7	3	−1
Temp °F	max	34	38	47	58	67	73	76	75	68	56	45	37
	min	25	28	30	42	50	56	60	59	53	44	37	30
Precipitation (mm)		39	44	44	45	70	67	84	72	42	56	52	45
Humidity %	am	81	80	78	72	74	74	74	78	83	86	84	84
	pm	72	66	57	49	52	55	54	54	56	64	74	76
Warsaw, Poland													
Temp °C	max	0	0	6	12	20	23	24	23	19	13	6	2
	min	−6	−6	−2	3	9	12	15	14	10	5	1	−3
Temp °F	max	32	32	42	53	67	73	75	73	66	55	42	35
	min	22	21	28	37	48	54	58	56	49	41	33	28
Precipitation (mm)		27	32	27	37	46	69	96	65	43	38	31	44
Humidity %	am	90	89	90	85	80	82	86	90	92	93	93	92
	pm	84	80	70	61	56	59	63	63	64	73	83	87
Yangon, Myanmar													
Temp °C	max	32	33	36	36	33	30	29	29	30	31	31	31
	min	18	19	22	24	25	24	24	24	24	24	23	19
Temp °F	max	89	92	96	97	92	86	85	85	86	88	88	88
	min	65	67	71	76	77	76	76	76	76	76	73	67
Precipitation (mm)		3	5	8	51	307	480	582	528	394	180	69	10
Humidity %	am	71	72	74	71	80	87	89	89	87	83	79	75
	pm	52	52	54	64	76	85	88	88	86	77	72	61
Zurich, Switzerland													
Temp °C	max	2	5	10	15	19	23	25	24	20	14	7	3
	min	−3	−2	1	4	8	12	14	13	11	6	2	−2
Temp °F	max	36	41	51	59	67	73	76	75	69	57	45	37
	min	26	28	34	40	47	53	56	56	51	43	35	29
Precipitation (mm)		74	69	64	76	101	129	136	124	102	77	73	64
Humidity %	am	88	88	86	81	80	80	81	85	90	92	90	89
	pm	74	65	55	51	52	52	52	53	57	64	73	76

Africa

Algeria **CAPITAL** Algiers **CURRENCY** Algerian dinar **DIALLING CODE** 213 **GMT** +1 **NATIONAL LANGUAGE** Arabic and French

Botswana **CAPITAL** Gaborone **CURRENCY** Pula **DIALLING CODE** 267 **GMT** +2 **NATIONAL LANGUAGE** English and Setswana

Egypt **CAPITAL** Cairo **CURRENCY** Egyptian pound **DIALLING CODE** 20 **GMT** +2 **NATIONAL LANGUAGE** Arabic

Ethiopia **CAPITAL** Addis Ababa **CURRENCY** Birr **DIALLING CODE** 251 **GMT** +3 **NATIONAL LANGUAGE** Amharic

Gambia **CAPITAL** Banjul **CURRENCY** Dalasi **DIALLING CODE** 220 **GMT** GMT **NATIONAL LANGUAGE** English

Kenya **CAPITAL** Nairobi **CURRENCY** Kenyan Shilling **DIALLING CODE** 254 **GMT** +3 **NATIONAL LANGUAGE** Swahili and English

Libya **CAPITAL** Tripoli **CURRENCY** Libyan dinar **DIALLING CODE** 218 **GMT** +1 **NATIONAL LANGUAGE** Arabic

Madagascar **CAPITAL** Antananarivo **CURRENCY** Malagasy franc **DIALLING CODE** 261 **GMT** +3 **NATIONAL LANGUAGE** Malagasy and French

Malawi **CAPITAL** Lilongwe **CURRENCY** Kwacha **DIALLING CODE** 265 **GMT** +2 **NATIONAL LANGUAGE** English

Mali **CAPITAL** Bamako **CURRENCY** CFA franc **DIALLING CODE** 223 **GMT** +2 **NATIONAL LANGUAGE** French

Morocco **CAPITAL** Rabat **CURRENCY** Dirham **DIALLING CODE** 212 **GMT** GMT **NATIONAL LANGUAGE** Arabic

Mozambique **CAPITAL** Maputo **CURRENCY** Mozambique metical **DIALLING CODE** 258 **GMT** +2 **NATIONAL LANGUAGE** Portuguese

Namibia CAPITAL Windhoek CURRENCY South African rand
DIALLING CODE 264 GMT +2 NATIONAL LANGUAGE English

Rwanda CAPITAL Kigali CURRENCY Rwandese franc DIALLING CODE 250
GMT +2 NATIONAL LANGUAGE Kinyarwanda and French

Senegal CAPITAL Dakar CURRENCY CFA DIALLING CODE 221
GMT GMT NATIONAL LANGUAGE French and Wolof

Seychelles CAPITAL Victoria on Mahe CURRENCY Seychelles rupee
DIALLING CODE 248 GMT +4 NATIONAL LANGUAGE Creole

South Africa CAPITAL Pretoria CURRENCY Rand DIALLING CODE 27
GMT +2 NATIONAL LANGUAGE English and Afrikaans

Sudan CAPITAL Khartoum CURRENCY Sudanese pound DIALLING
CODE 249 GMT +2 NATIONAL LANGUAGE Arabic

Tanzania CAPITAL Dodoma CURRENCY Tanzanian shilling DIALLING
CODE 255 GMT +3 NATIONAL LANGUAGE English and Swahili

Tunisia CAPITAL Tunis CURRENCY Tunisian dinar DIALLING CODE 216
GMT +1 NATIONAL LANGUAGE Arabic

Uganda CAPITAL Kampala CURRENCY Uganda shilling DIALLING
CODE 256 GMT +3 NATIONAL LANGUAGE English

Zambia CAPITAL Lusaka CURRENCY Kwacha DIALLING CODE 260
GMT +2 NATIONAL LANGUAGE English

Zimbabwe CAPITAL Harare CURRENCY Zimbabwe dollar DIALLING
CODE 263 GMT +2 NATIONAL LANGUAGE English

Americas & the Caribbean

Argentina CAPITAL Buenos Aires CURRENCY Argentine peso
DIALLING CODE 54 GMT −3 NATIONAL LANGUAGE Spanish

COUNTRY FACTS

Bahamas CAPITAL Nassau CURRENCY Bahamian dollar DIALLING CODE 1 242 GMT −5 NATIONAL LANGUAGE English

Barbuda CAPITAL St John's CURRENCY Eastern Caribbean dollar DIALLING CODE 1 268 GMT −4 NATIONAL LANGUAGE English

Bolivia CAPITAL La Paz CURRENCY Boliviano DIALLING CODE 591 GMT −4 NATIONAL LANGUAGE Spanish

Brazil CAPITAL Brasilia CURRENCY Cruzeiro DIALLING CODE 55 GMT −3/−5 NATIONAL LANGUAGE Portuguese

British Virgin Islands CAPITAL Road Town CURRENCY US dollar DIALLING CODE 1 284 GMT −4 NATIONAL LANGUAGE English

Canada CAPITAL Ottawa CURRENCY Canadian dollar DIALLING CODE 1 GMT −3.5/−8 NATIONAL LANGUAGE English and French

Chile CAPITAL Santiago CURRENCY Peso DIALLING CODE 56 GMT −6 NATIONAL LANGUAGE Spanish

Colombia CAPITAL Bogota CURRENCY Peso DIALLING CODE 57 GMT −5 NATIONAL LANGUAGE Spanish

Cuba CAPITAL Havana CURRENCY Cuban peso DIALLING CODE 53 GMT −4 NATIONAL LANGUAGE Spanish

Ecuador CAPITAL Quito CURRENCY Sucre DIALLING CODE 593 GMT −5 NATIONAL LANGUAGE Spanish

Grenada CAPITAL St Georges CURRENCY Eastern Caribbean dollar DIALLING CODE 1 473 GMT −4 NATIONAL LANGUAGE English

Jamaica CAPITAL Kingston CURRENCY Jamaican dollar DIALLING CODE 1 876 GMT −5 NATIONAL LANGUAGE English

Mexico CAPITAL Mexico City CURRENCY Peso DIALLING CODE 52 GMT −6/−8 NATIONAL LANGUAGE Spanish

Peru **CAPITAL** Lima **CURRENCY** Nuevo sol **DIALLING CODE** 51 **GMT** −5 **NATIONAL LANGUAGE** Spanish and Quechua

Saba **CAPITAL** The Bottom **CURRENCY** Netherlands Antilles guilder **DIALLING CODE** 1 599 **GMT** −4 **NATIONAL LANGUAGE** English and Dutch

USA **CAPITAL** Washington DC **CURRENCY** US dollar **DIALLING CODE** 1 **GMT** −5/−10 **NATIONAL LANGUAGE** English

Venezuela **CAPITAL** Caracas **CURRENCY** Bolivar **DIALLING CODE** 58 **GMT** −4 **NATIONAL LANGUAGE** Spanish

Asia

Afghanistan **CAPITAL** Kabul **CURRENCY** Afgani **DIALLING CODE** 93 **GMT** +4.5 **NATIONAL LANGUAGE** Pashtu and Dari

Cambodia **CAPITAL** Phnom Penh **CURRENCY** Riel **DIALLING CODE** 855 **GMT** +7 **NATIONAL LANGUAGE** Khmer

China **CAPITAL** Beijing **CURRENCY** Yuan **DIALLING CODE** 86 **GMT** +8 **NATIONAL LANGUAGE** Mandarin Chinese

India **CAPITAL** New Delhi **CURRENCY** Rupee **DIALLING CODE** 91 **GMT** +5.5 **NATIONAL LANGUAGE** English

Indonesia **CAPITAL** Jakarta **CURRENCY** Rupiah **DIALLING CODE** 62 **GMT** +7/+9 **NATIONAL LANGUAGE** Bahasa Indonesian

Japan **CAPITAL** Tokyo **CURRENCY** Japanese yen **DIALLING CODE** 81 **GMT** +9 **NATIONAL LANGUAGE** Japanese

Laos **CAPITAL** Vientiane **CURRENCY** Lao Kip **DIALLING CODE** 856 **GMT** +7 **NATIONAL LANGUAGE** Laotian

Malaysia **CAPITAL** Kuala Lumpur **CURRENCY** Ringgit **DIALLING CODE** 60 **GMT** +8 **NATIONAL LANGUAGE** Bahasa Malaysian

COUNTRY FACTS

Myanmar CAPITAL Naypyidaw CURRENCY Kyat DIALLING CODE 95
GMT +6.5 NATIONAL LANGUAGE Burmese

Nepal CAPITAL Kathmandu CURRENCY Nepalese rupee DIALLING
CODE 977 GMT +5.5 NATIONAL LANGUAGE Nepali

Philippines CAPITAL Manila CURRENCY Philippine peso DIALLING
CODE 63 GMT +8 NATIONAL LANGUAGE Filipino

Sri Lanka CAPITAL Colombo CURRENCY Sri Lankan rupee DIALLING
CODE 94 GMT +5.5 NATIONAL LANGUAGE Sinhala, Tamil and English

Thailand CAPITAL Bangkok CURRENCY Baht DIALLING CODE 66
GMT +7 NATIONAL LANGUAGE Thai

Uzbekistan CAPITAL Tashkent CURRENCY Som DIALLING CODE 998
GMT +5 NATIONAL LANGUAGE Uzbek

Vietnam CAPITAL Hanoi CURRENCY Dong DIALLING CODE 84 GMT +7
NATIONAL LANGUAGE Vietnamese

Australasia & Oceania

Australia CAPITAL Canberra CURRENCY Australian dollar DIALLING
CODE 61 GMT +8/+10 NATIONAL LANGUAGE English

Cook Islands CAPITAL Avarua CURRENCY New Zealand dollar
DIALLING CODE 682 GMT −10 NATIONAL LANGUAGE Maori and English

French Polynesia CAPITAL Papeete CURRENCY French Pacific franc
DIALLING CODE 689 GMT −9/−10 NATIONAL LANGUAGE Tahitian and French

New Zealand CAPITAL Wellington CURRENCY New Zealand dollar
DIALLING CODE 64 GMT +12 NATIONAL LANGUAGE English

Europe & the Middle East

Austria CAPITAL Vienna CURRENCY Euro DIALLING CODE 43 GMT +1
NATIONAL LANGUAGE German

Belarus CAPITAL Minsk CURRENCY Belarussian rubel DIALLING
CODE 375 GMT +2 NATIONAL LANGUAGE Belarussian

Belgium CAPITAL Brussels CURRENCY Euro DIALLING CODE 32 GMT +1
NATIONAL LANGUAGE Flemish and French

Bulgaria CAPITAL Sofia CURRENCY Lev DIALLING CODE 359 GMT +2
NATIONAL LANGUAGE Bulgarian

Croatia CAPITAL Zagreb CURRENCY Croatian dinar DIALLING CODE 385
GMT +1 NATIONAL LANGUAGE Croatian

Czech Republic CAPITAL Prague CURRENCY Koruna DIALLING
CODE 420 GMT +1 NATIONAL LANGUAGE Czech

Denmark CAPITAL Copenhagen CURRENCY Danish Krone DIALLING
CODE 45 GMT +1 NATIONAL LANGUAGE Danish

Estonia CAPITAL Tallinn CURRENCY Kroon DIALLING CODE 372 GMT +2
NATIONAL LANGUAGE Estonian

Finland CAPITAL Helsinki CURRENCY Euro DIALLING CODE 358 GMT +2
NATIONAL LANGUAGE Finnish

France CAPITAL Paris CURRENCY Euro DIALLING CODE 33 GMT +1
NATIONAL LANGUAGE French

Germany CAPITAL Berlin CURRENCY Euro DIALLING CODE 49 GMT +1
NATIONAL LANGUAGE German

Greece CAPITAL Athens CURRENCY Euro DIALLING CODE 30 GMT +2
NATIONAL LANGUAGE Greek

COUNTRY FACTS

Hungary **CAPITAL** Budapest **CURRENCY** Forint **DIALLING CODE** 36 **GMT** +1 **NATIONAL LANGUAGE** Hungarian

Iran **CAPITAL** Tehran **CURRENCY** Iranian rial **DIALLING CODE** 98 **GMT** +3.5 **NATIONAL LANGUAGE** Persian (Farsi)

Ireland **CAPITAL** Dublin **CURRENCY** Euro **DIALLING CODE** 353 **GMT** GMT **NATIONAL LANGUAGE** English and Gaelic

Israel **CAPITAL** Jerusalem **CURRENCY** New Israeli Sheqel **DIALLING CODE** 972 **GMT** +2 **NATIONAL LANGUAGE** Hebrew and Arabic

Italy **CAPITAL** Rome **CURRENCY** Euro **DIALLING CODE** 39 **GMT** +1 **NATIONAL LANGUAGE** Italian

Jordan **CAPITAL** Amman **CURRENCY** Dinar **DIALLING CODE** 962 **GMT** +2 **NATIONAL LANGUAGE** Arabic

Latvia **CAPITAL** Riga **CURRENCY** Latvian lat **DIALLING CODE** 371 **GMT** +2 **NATIONAL LANGUAGE** Latvian

Macedonia **CAPITAL** Skopje **CURRENCY** Macedonian denar **DIALLING CODE** 389 **GMT** +1 **NATIONAL LANGUAGE** Macedonian

Malta **CAPITAL** Valletta **CURRENCY** Euro **DIALLING CODE** 356 **GMT** +1 **NATIONAL LANGUAGE** Maltese

Montenegro **CAPITAL** Podgorica **CURRENCY** Euro **DIALLING CODE** 382 **GMT** +1 **NATIONAL LANGUAGE** Montenegrin

Netherlands **CAPITAL** Amsterdam **CURRENCY** Euro **DIALLING CODE** 31 **GMT** +1 **NATIONAL LANGUAGE** Dutch

Norway **CAPITAL** Oslo **CURRENCY** Norwegian krone **DIALLING CODE** 47 **GMT** +1 **NATIONAL LANGUAGE** Norwegian

Poland **CAPITAL** Warsaw **CURRENCY** Zloty **DIALLING CODE** 48 **GMT** +1 **NATIONAL LANGUAGE** Polish

Portugal **CAPITAL** Lisbon **CURRENCY** Euro **DIALLING CODE** 351
GMT GMT **NATIONAL LANGUAGE** Portuguese

Romania **CAPITAL** Bucharest **CURRENCY** Leu **DIALLING CODE** 40
GMT +2 **NATIONAL LANGUAGE** Romanian

Russia **CAPITAL** Moscow **CURRENCY** Ruble **DIALLING CODE** 7
GMT +3/+12 **NATIONAL LANGUAGE** Russian

Slovakia **CAPITAL** Bratislava **CURRENCY** Koruna **DIALLING CODE** 421
GMT +1 **NATIONAL LANGUAGE** Slovak

Slovenia **CAPITAL** Ljubljana **CURRENCY** Euro **DIALLING CODE** 386
GMT +1 **NATIONAL LANGUAGE** Slovene

Spain **CAPITAL** Madrid **CURRENCY** Euro **DIALLING CODE** 34 **GMT** +1
NATIONAL LANGUAGE Spanish

Sweden **CAPITAL** Stockholm **CURRENCY** Swedish Krona **DIALLING
CODE** 46 **GMT** +1 **NATIONAL LANGUAGE** Swedish

Switzerland **CAPITAL** Bern **CURRENCY** Swiss franc **DIALLING
CODE** 41 **GMT** +1 **NATIONAL LANGUAGE** German, French and Italian

Syria **CAPITAL** Damascus **CURRENCY** Syrian pound **DIALLING CODE** 963
GMT +2 **NATIONAL LANGUAGE** Arabic, French and English

Turkey **CAPITAL** Ankara **CURRENCY** Turkish lire **DIALLING CODE** 90
GMT +2 **NATIONAL LANGUAGE** Turkish

Ukraine **CAPITAL** Kiev **CURRENCY** Hryvnia **DIALLING CODE** 380 **GMT** +2
NATIONAL LANGUAGE Ukrainian

United Kingdom **CAPITAL** London **CURRENCY** Pound **DIALLING
CODE** 44 **GMT** GMT **NATIONAL LANGUAGE** English

Yemen **CAPITAL** Sana'a **CURRENCY** Yemeni dinar **DIALLING CODE** 967
GMT +3 **NATIONAL LANGUAGE** Arabic

DESTIN

ATIONS

Star rating ☆ ☆ ☆ ☆ ☆

Destination:

DATE VISITED:

HIGHLIGHTS: _____

_____

_____

_____

_____

_____

NOTES: _____

_____

_____

_____

_____

_____

_____

_____

_____

_____

_____

_____

Did you know? *The area around Churchill, Manitoba in Canada is known as the polar bear capital of the world. In October and November, more than 1,200 bears gather to wait for Hudson Bay to freeze over so they can resume seal hunting. More than 10,000 visitors flock to see the bears.*

Star rating ☆ ☆ ☆ ☆ ☆

Destination:

DATE VISITED:

HIGHLIGHTS: _____

_____

_____

_____

_____

_____

NOTES: _____

_____

_____

_____

_____

_____

_____

_____

_____

_____

_____

Milford Sound, New Zealand

Star rating ☆ ☆ ☆ ☆ ☆

Destination:

DATE VISITED:

HIGHLIGHTS: _____

_____

_____

_____

_____

_____

NOTES: _____

_____

_____

_____

_____

_____

_____

_____

_____

_____

_____

_____

Did you know? *The oldest continuously inhabited city in the world is thought to be Damascus in Syria. Archaeological excavations in the city have uncovered evidence of human habitation dating back as far as 10,000 BC.*

Star rating ☆ ☆ ☆ ☆ ☆

Destination:

DATE VISITED:

HIGHLIGHTS: _____

_____

_____

_____

_____

_____

NOTES: _____

_____

_____

_____

_____

_____

_____

_____

_____

_____

_____

Star rating ☆ ☆ ☆ ☆ ☆

Destination:

DATE VISITED:

HIGHLIGHTS: _____

_____

_____

_____

_____

_____

NOTES: _____

_____

_____

_____

_____

_____

_____

_____

_____

_____

_____

Did you know? *The largest covered market in the world is the Grand Bazaar in Istanbul. With around 4,000 shops, it covers an impressive 20 ha (50 acres) and has been there since the 15th century, selling everything from spices and olives to jewellery, carpets and antiques.*

Star rating ☆ ☆ ☆ ☆ ☆

Destination:

DATE VISITED:

HIGHLIGHTS: _____

_____

_____

_____

_____

_____

NOTES: _____

_____

_____

_____

_____

_____

_____

_____

_____

_____

The Temple of Horus, Egypt

Destination:

DATE VISITED:

HIGHLIGHTS: _____

_____

_____

_____

_____

NOTES: _____

_____

_____

_____

_____

_____

_____

_____

_____

_____

Did you know?

The largest single religious monument in the world is Angkor Wat in Cambodia, built for King Suryavarman II in the early 12th century.

Star rating ☆ ☆ ☆ ☆ ☆

Destination:

DATE VISITED:

HIGHLIGHTS: _____

_____

_____

_____

_____

_____

NOTES: _____

_____

_____

_____

_____

_____

_____

_____

_____

_____

_____

_____

Destination:

DATE VISITED:

HIGHLIGHTS: _____

_____

_____

_____

_____

_____

NOTES: _____

_____

_____

_____

_____

_____

_____

_____

_____

_____

_____

_____

Did you know? *The world's first national park was Yellowstone in the USA, created by Ulysses S. Grant in 1872. The park is home to a diverse range of geysers, hot springs, mud pools and fumaroles. In fact, two-thirds of the world's geysers are in the park.*

Star rating  ☆ ☆ ☆ ☆ ☆

Destination:

DATE VISITED:

HIGHLIGHTS: _____

_____

_____

_____

_____

_____

NOTES: _____

_____

_____

_____

_____

_____

_____

_____

_____

_____

_____

Rangiroa, French Polynesia

Star rating ☆ ☆ ☆ ☆ ☆

Destination:

DATE VISITED:

HIGHLIGHTS: _____

_____

_____

_____

_____

_____

NOTES: _____

_____

_____

_____

_____

_____

_____

_____

_____

_____

_____

_____

_____

Did you know? *Between them the five Great Lakes of North America – Superior, Michigan, Huron, Erie and Ontario – contain more than 20 per cent of the world's fresh water. The combined surface area is larger than England, Scotland and Wales put together.*

Star rating ☆ ☆ ☆ ☆ ☆

Destination:

DATE VISITED:

HIGHLIGHTS: _____

_____

_____

_____

_____

_____

NOTES: _____

_____

_____

_____

_____

_____

_____

_____

_____

_____

_____

The Strip in Las Vegas

Destination:

DATE VISITED:

HIGHLIGHTS: _____

_____

_____

_____

_____

_____

NOTES: _____

_____

_____

_____

_____

_____

_____

_____

_____

_____

_____

_____

Did you know? *Some of the world's oldest trees are found on the Japanese island of Yakushima. The oldest of the Yaku cedars, known as Jomon Sugi, has a circumference of 16.4 m (54 ft) and is thought to be around 7,000 years old.*

Destination:

DATE VISITED:

HIGHLIGHTS: _____

_____

_____

_____

_____

_____

NOTES: _____

_____

_____

_____

_____

_____

_____

_____

_____

_____

_____

_____

Doors of the Royal Palace, Fès, Morocco

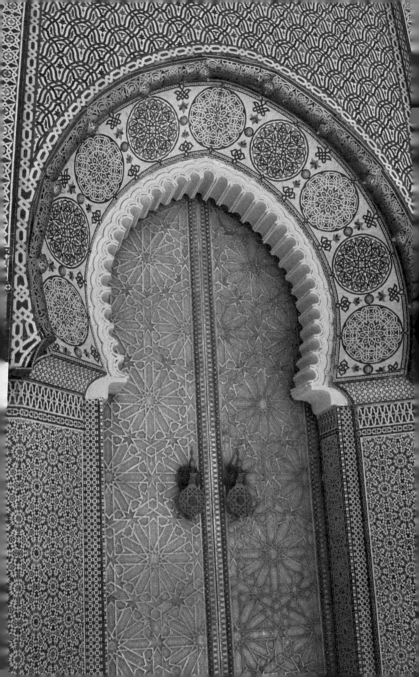

Star rating ☆ ☆ ☆ ☆ ☆

Destination:

DATE VISITED:

HIGHLIGHTS: _____

_____

_____

_____

_____

_____

NOTES: _____

_____

_____

_____

_____

_____

_____

_____

_____

_____

_____

_____

Did you know? *The largest UNESCO World Heritage Site is the Great Barrier Reef off the coast of Australia. It is also the most extensive coral reef system in the world, covering an area of 350,000 sq km (135,100 sq miles).*

Destination:

DATE VISITED:

HIGHLIGHTS: _____

_____

_____

_____

_____

_____

NOTES: _____

_____

_____

_____

_____

_____

_____

_____

_____

_____

_____

Destination:

DATE VISITED:

HIGHLIGHTS: _____

_____

_____

_____

_____

_____

NOTES: _____

_____

_____

_____

_____

_____

_____

_____

_____

_____

_____

_____

_____

Did you know? *The world's oldest tourist attraction is the Pyramid complex at Giza near Cairo, featuring three enormous pyramids and the Sphinx. The pyramids are the only one of the Seven Wonders of the Ancient World still in existence.*

Star rating ☆ ☆ ☆ ☆ ☆

Destination:

DATE VISITED:

HIGHLIGHTS: _____

_____

_____

_____

_____

_____

NOTES: _____

_____

_____

_____

_____

_____

_____

_____

_____

_____

_____

Salzburg, Austria

Star rating ☆ ☆ ☆ ☆ ☆

Destination:

DATE VISITED:

HIGHLIGHTS: _____

_____

_____

_____

_____

_____

NOTES: _____

_____

_____

_____

_____

_____

_____

_____

_____

_____

_____

_____

Did you know? *Easter Island is one of the most isolated places on earth. Lying about half way between Tahiti and coastal Chile in the South Pacific, the island is more than 3,219 km (2,000 miles) from an area of any significant population. Easter island is famous for its giant stone statues.*

Star rating ☆ ☆ ☆ ☆ ☆

Destination:

DATE VISITED:

HIGHLIGHTS: _____

_____

_____

_____

_____

_____

NOTES: _____

_____

_____

_____

_____

_____

_____

_____

_____

_____

_____

_____

The statues of Easter Island

Star rating ☆ ☆ ☆ ☆ ☆

Destination:

DATE VISITED:

HIGHLIGHTS: _____

_____

_____

_____

_____

NOTES: _____

_____

_____

_____

_____

_____

_____

_____

_____

_____

_____

Did you know?

The spray produced by the majestic Victoria Falls in Zambia can be seen 64 km (40 miles) away. The water plummets over a sheer drop of 100 m (330 ft) into a deep gorge below.

Destination:

DATE VISITED:

HIGHLIGHTS: _____

_____

_____

_____

_____

NOTES: _____

_____

_____

_____

_____

_____

_____

_____

_____

_____

The magnificent Taj Mahal is more a work of art than a mausoleum.

Destination:

DATE VISITED:

HIGHLIGHTS: _____

_____

_____

_____

_____

_____

NOTES: _____

_____

_____

_____

_____

_____

_____

_____

_____

_____

_____

_____

Did you know? *The Isle of Gorée off the coast of Senegal was the largest slave trade centre on the African coast between the 15th and 19th centuries. An estimated 40 million Africans were held here as they awaited passage to the Americas.*

Destination:

DATE VISITED:

HIGHLIGHTS: _____

_____

_____

_____

_____

_____

NOTES: _____

_____

_____

_____

_____

_____

_____

_____

_____

_____

_____

_____

_____

Star rating ☆ ☆ ☆ ☆ ☆

Destination:

DATE VISITED:

HIGHLIGHTS: _____

_____

_____

_____

_____

_____

NOTES: _____

_____

_____

_____

_____

_____

_____

_____

_____

_____

_____

Did you know? The largest annual rodeo in North America is the Calgary Stampede. This prestigious event is a rowdy occasion with competitions for riding bucking broncos and bulls, calf roping and steer wrestling. This is the real thing!

Star rating ☆ ☆ ☆ ☆ ☆

Destination:

DATE VISITED:

HIGHLIGHTS: _____

_____

_____

_____

_____

NOTES: _____

_____

_____

_____

_____

_____

_____

_____

_____

_____

_____

Eilean Donan Castle, Loch Duich, Scotland

Star rating  ☆ ☆ ☆ ☆ ☆

Destination:

DATE VISITED:

HIGHLIGHTS: _____

_____

_____

_____

_____

_____

NOTES: _____

_____

_____

_____

_____

_____

_____

_____

_____

_____

_____

_____

Did you know? *The Great Wall of China, one of the largest man-made structures in the world, runs for about 6,700 km (4,163 miles) from East to West. This 8 m (26 ft) thick wall was started in the 8th century BC as a military fortification.*

Destination:

DATE VISITED:

HIGHLIGHTS: _____

_____

_____

_____

_____

_____

NOTES: _____

_____

_____

_____

_____

_____

_____

_____

_____

_____

_____

_____

Ulugh Beg and Sherdar madrasahs in the Registan, Samarkand, Uzbekistan

Star rating ☆ ☆ ☆ ☆ ☆

Destination:

DATE VISITED:

HIGHLIGHTS: _____

_____

_____

_____

_____

_____

NOTES: _____

_____

_____

_____

_____

_____

_____

_____

_____

_____

_____

_____

_____

Did you know? The most visited game reserve in Africa is the Masai Mara, covering around 1,510 sq km (938 sq miles) of plains and woodlands. The reserve, found in south-west Kenya, contains the richest and most varied wildlife of any park on the continent.

Star rating

Destination:

DATE VISITED:

HIGHLIGHTS: _____

_____

_____

_____

_____

_____

NOTES: _____

_____

_____

_____

_____

_____

_____

_____

_____

_____

_____

_____

The Colosseum in Rome, Italy

Destination:

DATE VISITED:

HIGHLIGHTS: _____

_____

_____

_____

_____

_____

NOTES: _____

_____

_____

_____

_____

_____

_____

_____

_____

_____

_____

_____

Did you know? *Iguazú Falls in Argentina are higher and nearly twice as wide as the famous falls at Niagara. The most spectacular part of the falls is the Devil's Throat, a U-shaped cliff with a fall of water 150 m (492 ft) wide and 700 m (2,297 ft) tall.*

Star rating ☆ ☆ ☆ ☆ ☆

Destination:

DATE VISITED:

HIGHLIGHTS: _____

_____

_____

_____

_____

_____

NOTES: _____

_____

_____

_____

_____

_____

_____

_____

_____

_____

_____

_____

View from trail on Ko Wua Ta Lap Ang Thong National Marine Park, Thailand

Star rating ☆ ☆ ☆ ☆ ☆

Destination:

DATE VISITED:

HIGHLIGHTS: _____

_____

_____

_____

_____

_____

NOTES: _____

_____

_____

_____

_____

_____

_____

_____

_____

_____

_____

Did you know? The world's largest unbroken caldera is Ngorongoro in Tanzania. The crater is 610 m (2,001 ft) deep and covers an area of 260 sq km (162 sq miles). Millions of years ago the mountain was roughly the same size as Mount Kilimanjaro but as volcanic activity subsided the mountain collapsed to leave the caldera.

Star rating ☆ ☆ ☆ ☆ ☆

Destination:

DATE VISITED:

HIGHLIGHTS: _____

_____

_____

_____

_____

_____

NOTES: _____

_____

_____

_____

_____

_____

_____

_____

_____

_____

_____

Prayer flags at the Saga Dawa Festival, Tibet

Destination:

DATE VISITED:

HIGHLIGHTS: _____

_____

_____

_____

_____

_____

NOTES: _____

_____

_____

_____

_____

_____

_____

_____

_____

_____

_____

Did you know? *The Schwedagon Paya, a Buddhist stupa in Yangon, is decorated with pure gold and the upper reaches are encrusted with diamonds and rubies. The bell-shaped monument is, not surprisingly, one of the most impressive in Myanmar.*

Destination:

DATE VISITED:

HIGHLIGHTS: _____

_____

_____

_____

_____

_____

NOTES: _____

_____

_____

_____

_____

_____

_____

_____

_____

_____

_____

Cherry blossom at the Kiyomizu-dera, Kyoto, Japan

Destination:

DATE VISITED:

HIGHLIGHTS: _____

_____

_____

_____

_____

_____

NOTES: _____ _____

_____

_____

_____

_____

_____

_____

_____

_____

_____

_____

_____

Did you know? *The largest Chinese community outside China is in San Francisco. The area, known not surprisingly as China Town, is accessed through ornate and colourful gates on Stockton and Bush streets.*

Destination:

DATE VISITED:

HIGHLIGHTS: _____

_____

_____

_____

_____

_____

NOTES: _____

_____

_____

_____

_____

_____

_____

_____

_____

_____

_____

Star rating ☆ ☆ ☆ ☆ ☆

Destination:

DATE VISITED:

HIGHLIGHTS: _____

_____

_____

_____

_____

_____

NOTES: _____

_____

_____

_____

_____

_____

_____

_____

_____

_____

_____

_____

Did you know? *The largest inland delta in the world is the Okavango Delta in the middle of the Kalahari Desert. The Okavango River originates in the uplands of Angola, then spreads across the sandy Kalahari on its way to Botswana, creating a vast delta with labyrinthine channels and palm-fringed islands.*

Star rating ☆ ☆ ☆ ☆ ☆

Destination:

DATE VISITED:

HIGHLIGHTS: _____

_____

_____

_____

_____

_____

NOTES: _____

_____

_____

_____

_____

_____

_____

_____

_____

_____

_____

_____

The Rockies tower over Vancouver, Canada

Star rating ☆ ☆ ☆ ☆ ☆

Destination:

DATE VISITED:

HIGHLIGHTS: _____

_____

_____

_____

_____

_____

NOTES: _____

_____

_____

_____

_____

_____

_____

_____

_____

_____

_____

Did you know? *The largest and deepest caldera lake in the world is Lake Toba in Indonesia. Created more than 74,000 years ago by a volcanic eruption, the caldera is high in the treeless mountains of northern Sumatra and covers an area of 1,707 sq km (436 sq miles) with a depth of 529 m (1,735 ft).*

Destination:

DATE VISITED:

HIGHLIGHTS: _____

_____

_____

_____

_____

_____

NOTES: _____

_____

_____

_____

_____

_____

_____

_____

_____

_____

_____

Destination:

DATE VISITED:

HIGHLIGHTS: _____

_____

_____

_____

_____

_____

NOTES: _____

_____

_____

_____

_____

_____

_____

_____

_____

_____

_____

Did you know? *The oldest city in the United States is St Augustin in Florida. It was founded by the Spanish admiral Pedro Menéndez de Avilés in 1565. The huge fortified Castillo de San Marcos, built from 1672–95, served as a Spanish outpost and remains intact today.*

Star rating ☆ ☆ ☆ ☆ ☆

Destination:

DATE VISITED:

HIGHLIGHTS: _____

_____

_____

_____

_____

_____

NOTES: _____

_____

_____

_____

_____

_____

_____

_____

_____

_____

_____

Star rating ☆ ☆ ☆ ☆ ☆

Destination:

DATE VISITED:

HIGHLIGHTS: _____
_____
_____
_____
_____
_____

NOTES: _____
_____
_____
_____
_____
_____
_____
_____
_____
_____
_____
_____
_____

Did you know? *The largest game park in Kenya, and the most popular destination for African safaris, is Tsavo National Park. At just over 21,000 sq km (10 million acres), the park is larger than Jamaica and is best known for its high concentrations of elephants and lions.*

Star rating ☆ ☆ ☆ ☆ ☆

Destination:

DATE VISITED:

HIGHLIGHTS: _____

_____

_____

_____

_____

_____

NOTES: _____

_____

_____

_____

_____

_____

_____

_____

_____

_____

_____

Fishermen using cormorants to fish on the Li River, Guilin, China.

Destination:

DATE VISITED:

HIGHLIGHTS: _____

_____

_____

_____

_____

_____

NOTES: _____

_____

_____

_____

_____

_____

_____

_____

_____

_____

_____

_____

Did you know? *The Forbidden City in Beijing is the grandest and best preserved imperial palace in the world. The complex has 9,999 buildings covering an area of 74 ha (183 acres). It is surrounded by a 6-m (20-ft) deep moat and a 10-m (33-ft) high wall.*

Star rating ☆ ☆ ☆ ☆ ☆

Destination:

DATE VISITED:

HIGHLIGHTS: _____

_____

_____

_____

_____

_____

NOTES: _____

_____

_____

_____

_____

_____

_____

_____

_____

_____

_____

_____

Destination:

DATE VISITED:

HIGHLIGHTS: _____

_____

_____

_____

_____

_____

NOTES: _____

_____

_____

_____

_____

_____

_____

_____

_____

_____

_____

_____

Did you know? *The oldest desert on earth is the Namib Desert in Namiba, which also features some of the highest sand dunes in the world. This ancient desert, with its 300 m (762 ft) red and grey sand dunes, stretches along 1,600 km (1,000 miles) of barren coastline.*

Star rating ☆ ☆ ☆ ☆ ☆

Destination:

DATE VISITED:

HIGHLIGHTS: _____

_____

_____

_____

_____

_____

NOTES: _____

_____

_____

_____

_____

_____

_____

_____

_____

_____

_____

_____

The stunning dunes of the Namib Desert

Star rating ☆ ☆ ☆ ☆ ☆

Destination:

DATE VISITED:

HIGHLIGHTS: _____

_____

_____

_____

_____

_____

NOTES: _____

_____

_____

_____

_____

_____

_____

_____

_____

_____

_____

_____

Did you know? *The famous Blue Lagoon where Brook Shields was ship-wrecked in the 1980s film is in fact near Port Antonio in Jamaica. This idyllic spot, with emerald and turquoise waters, is still an unspoilt oasis.*

Star rating ☆ ☆ ☆ ☆ ☆

Destination:

DATE VISITED:

HIGHLIGHTS: _____

_____

_____

_____

_____

_____

NOTES: _____

_____

_____

_____

_____

_____

_____

_____

_____

_____

_____

_____

Star rating ☆ ☆ ☆ ☆ ☆

Destination:

DATE VISITED:

HIGHLIGHTS: _____

_____

_____

_____

_____

_____

NOTES: _____

_____

_____

_____

_____

_____

_____

_____

_____

_____

_____

_____

_____

_____

_____

_____

_____

_____

_____

_____

_____

_____

_____

_____

_____

_____

_____

_____

_____

Did you know? *There is a foliage hot line which visitors can telephone to give them hour-by-hour reports of the best places to view colourful autumn foliage in New England, USA.*

Star rating ☆ ☆ ☆ ☆ ☆

Destination:

DATE VISITED:

HIGHLIGHTS: _____

_____

_____

_____

_____

_____

NOTES: _____

_____

_____

_____

_____

_____

_____

_____

_____

_____

_____

_____

Star rating  ☆ ☆ ☆ ☆ ☆

Destination:

DATE VISITED:

HIGHLIGHTS: _____

_____

_____

_____

_____

_____

NOTES: _____

_____

_____

_____

_____

_____

_____

_____

_____

_____

_____

_____

Did you know? It is through a quirk of evolution that no predators evolved on the Galapagos Islands, so the rich and varied fauna there, including the famous giant tortoises, have no fear, not even of man, which makes this a wonderful place for wildlife watching.

Star rating ☆ ☆ ☆ ☆ ☆

Destination:

DATE VISITED:

HIGHLIGHTS: _____

_____

_____

_____

_____

_____

NOTES: _____

_____

_____

_____

_____

_____

_____

_____

_____

_____

_____

_____

Autumn colours at Lac Monroe in the Laurentians, Canada

Star rating ☆ ☆ ☆ ☆ ☆

Destination:

DATE VISITED:

HIGHLIGHTS: _____

_____

_____

_____

_____

_____

NOTES: _____

_____

_____

_____

_____

_____

_____

_____

_____

_____

_____

_____

Did you know? The Dead Sea is the largest hypersaline lake in the world, located at the lowest exposed point on the earth's surface on the border between the West Bank, Israel and Jordan. The high salt content means no fish or other aquatic organisms can live in it, although there are small amounts of bacteria and fungi.

Star rating ☆ ☆ ☆ ☆ ☆

Destination:

DATE VISITED:

HIGHLIGHTS: _____

_____

_____

_____

_____

_____

NOTES: _____

_____

_____

_____

_____

_____

_____

_____

_____

_____

_____

Star rating ☆ ☆ ☆ ☆ ☆

Destination:

DATE VISITED:

HIGHLIGHTS: _____

_____

_____

_____

_____

_____

NOTES: _____

_____

_____

_____

_____

_____

_____

_____

_____

_____

_____

Did you know? *One of the biggest and best preserved medinas in the Arab world is at Sana'a in Yemen. The old walled city has over 50,000 inhabitants, many of them living in houses over 400 years old. The world's oldest high-rise buildings are found here, six- and seven-storey houses built of black basalt and mud bricks.*

Star rating ☆ ☆ ☆ ☆ ☆

Destination:

DATE VISITED:

HIGHLIGHTS: _____

_____

_____

_____

_____

_____

NOTES: _____

_____

_____

_____

_____

_____

_____

_____

_____

_____

_____

_____

The Old Medina at Chefchaouen, Morocco

sketches
PHO

TOS
thoughts

addre

SS
BOOK

ADDRESS BOOK

Name:

ADDRESS:

TEL: **EMAIL:**

Name:

ADDRESS:

TEL: **EMAIL:**

Name:

ADDRESS:

TEL: **EMAIL:**

Name:

ADDRESS:

TEL: **EMAIL:**

Name:

ADDRESS:

TEL: **EMAIL:**

Name:

ADDRESS:

TEL: **EMAIL:**

Name:

ADDRESS:

TEL: **EMAIL:**

Name:

ADDRESS:

TEL: **EMAIL:**

Name:

ADDRESS:

TEL: **EMAIL:**

Name:

ADDRESS:

TEL: **EMAIL:**

ADDRESS BOOK

Name:

ADDRESS:

TEL: **EMAIL:**

Name:

ADDRESS:

TEL: **EMAIL:**

Name:

ADDRESS:

TEL: **EMAIL:**

Name:

ADDRESS:

TEL: **EMAIL:**

Name:

ADDRESS:

TEL: **EMAIL:**

Name:

ADDRESS:

TEL: **EMAIL:**

Name:

ADDRESS:

TEL: **EMAIL:**

Name:

ADDRESS:

TEL: **EMAIL:**

Name:

ADDRESS:

TEL: **EMAIL:**

Name:

ADDRESS:

TEL: **EMAIL:**

ADDRESS BOOK

Name:

ADDRESS:

TEL: **EMAIL:**

Name:

ADDRESS:

TEL: **EMAIL:**

Name:

ADDRESS:

TEL: **EMAIL:**

Name:

ADDRESS:

TEL: **EMAIL:**

Name:

ADDRESS:

TEL: **EMAIL:**

Giant redwoods in Humboldt County, California, USA

ADDRESS BOOK

Name:

ADDRESS:

TEL: **EMAIL:**

Name:

ADDRESS:

TEL: **EMAIL:**

Name:

ADDRESS:

TEL: **EMAIL:**

Name:

ADDRESS:

TEL: **EMAIL:**

Name:

ADDRESS:

TEL: **EMAIL:**

Name:

ADDRESS:

TEL: **EMAIL:**

Name:

ADDRESS:

TEL: **EMAIL:**

Name:

ADDRESS:

TEL: **EMAIL:**

Name:

ADDRESS:

TEL: **EMAIL:**

Name:

ADDRESS:

TEL: **EMAIL:**

ADDRESS BOOK

Name:

ADDRESS:

TEL: **EMAIL:**

Name:

ADDRESS:

TEL: **EMAIL:**

Name:

ADDRESS:

TEL: **EMAIL:**

Name:

ADDRESS:

TEL: **EMAIL:**

Name:

ADDRESS:

TEL: **EMAIL:**

The gilded domes of the Annunciation Cathedral, Moscow, Russia

ADDRESS BOOK

Name:

ADDRESS:

TEL: **EMAIL:**

Name:

ADDRESS:

TEL: **EMAIL:**

Name:

ADDRESS:

TEL: **EMAIL:**

Name:

ADDRESS:

TEL: **EMAIL:**

Name:

ADDRESS:

TEL: **EMAIL:**

Name:

ADDRESS:

TEL: **EMAIL:**

Name:

ADDRESS:

TEL: **EMAIL:**

Name:

ADDRESS:

TEL: **EMAIL:**

Name:

ADDRESS:

TEL: **EMAIL:**

Name:

ADDRESS:

TEL: **EMAIL:**

ADDRESS BOOK

Name: _____

ADDRESS: _____

_____

TEL: _____ **EMAIL:** _____

Name: _____

ADDRESS: _____

_____

TEL: _____ **EMAIL:** _____

Name: _____

ADDRESS: _____

_____

TEL: _____ **EMAIL:** _____

Name: _____

ADDRESS: _____

_____

TEL: _____ **EMAIL:** _____

Name: _____

ADDRESS: _____

_____

TEL: _____ **EMAIL:** _____

The Treasury, Petra's most impressive monument

ADDRESS BOOK

Name:

ADDRESS:

TEL: **EMAIL:**

Name:

ADDRESS:

TEL: **EMAIL:**

Name:

ADDRESS:

TEL: **EMAIL:**

Name:

ADDRESS:

TEL: **EMAIL:**

Name:

ADDRESS:

TEL: **EMAIL:**

Name:

ADDRESS:

TEL: **EMAIL:**

Name:

ADDRESS:

TEL: **EMAIL:**

Name:

ADDRESS:

TEL: **EMAIL:**

Name:

ADDRESS:

TEL: **EMAIL:**

Name:

ADDRESS:

TEL: **EMAIL:**

ADDRESS BOOK

Name:

ADDRESS:

TEL: **EMAIL:**

Name:

ADDRESS:

TEL: **EMAIL:**

Name:

ADDRESS:

TEL: **EMAIL:**

Name:

ADDRESS:

TEL: **EMAIL:**

Name:

ADDRESS:

TEL: **EMAIL:**

The Whitsunday Islands, Australia

ADDRESS BOOK

Name:

ADDRESS:

TEL: **EMAIL:**

Name:

ADDRESS:

TEL: **EMAIL:**

Name:

ADDRESS:

TEL: **EMAIL:**

Name:

ADDRESS:

TEL: **EMAIL:**

Name:

ADDRESS:

TEL: **EMAIL:**

Name:

ADDRESS:

TEL: **EMAIL:**

Name:

ADDRESS:

TEL: **EMAIL:**

Name:

ADDRESS:

TEL: **EMAIL:**

Name:

ADDRESS:

TEL: **EMAIL:**

Name:

ADDRESS:

TEL: **EMAIL:**

ADDRESS BOOK

Name:

ADDRESS:

TEL: **EMAIL:**

Name:

ADDRESS:

TEL: **EMAIL:**

Name:

ADDRESS:

TEL: **EMAIL:**

Name:

ADDRESS:

TEL: **EMAIL:**

Name:

ADDRESS:

TEL: **EMAIL:**

The Guggenheim Museum in Bilbao, Spain

ADDRESS BOOK

Name:

ADDRESS:

TEL: **EMAIL:**

Name:

ADDRESS:

TEL: **EMAIL:**

Name:

ADDRESS:

TEL: **EMAIL:**

Name:

ADDRESS:

TEL: **EMAIL:**

Name:

ADDRESS:

TEL: **EMAIL:**

Name:

ADDRESS:

TEL: **EMAIL:**

Name:

ADDRESS:

TEL: **EMAIL:**

Name:

ADDRESS:

TEL: **EMAIL:**

Name:

ADDRESS:

TEL: **EMAIL:**

Name:

ADDRESS:

TEL: **EMAIL:**

ADDRESS BOOK

Name:

ADDRESS:

TEL: **EMAIL:**

Name:

ADDRESS:

TEL: **EMAIL:**

Name:

ADDRESS:

TEL: **EMAIL:**

Name:

ADDRESS:

TEL: **EMAIL:**

Name:

ADDRESS:

TEL: **EMAIL:**

Name:

ADDRESS:

TEL: **EMAIL:**

Name:

ADDRESS:

TEL: **EMAIL:**

Name:

ADDRESS:

TEL: **EMAIL:**

Name:

ADDRESS:

TEL: **EMAIL:**

Name:

ADDRESS:

TEL: **EMAIL:**

CHEC

501

MUST-VISIT DESTINATIONS

KLIST

501 MUST-VISIT DESTINATIONS CHECKLIST

- [ ] **A**achen Cathedral, Germany
- [ ] A Coruña, Spain
- [ ] Acropolis, Greece
- [ ] Adam's Peak, Sri Lanka
- [ ] Aeolian Islands, Italy
- [ ] Agrigento, Italy
- [ ] Ait-Ben-Hadou, Morocco
- [ ] Aitutaki, Cook Islands
- [ ] Algonquin Provincial Park, Canada
- [ ] Alhambra, Spain
- [ ] Alpbach, Austria
- [ ] Amalfi Coast, Italy
- [ ] Ambalangoda, Sri Lanka
- [ ] Amboseli National Reserve, Kenya
- [ ] Amsterdam, Netherlands
- [ ] Anegada, British Virgin Islands
- [ ] Ang Thong Archipelago, Thailand
- [ ] Angkor, Cambodia
- [ ] Anuradhapura, Sri Lanka
- [ ] Arles, France
- [ ] Askum, Ethiopia
- [ ] Aso National Park, Japan
- [ ] Assisi, Italy
- [ ] Asuka, Japan
- [ ] Aswan, Egypt
- [ ] Aurora Borealis, seen from Norway
- [ ] Auschwitz concentration camp, Poland
- [ ] Aven-Armand Cave, France
- [ ] Avignon, France
- [ ] Ayutthaya, Thailand
- [ ] **B**aalbek, Jordan
- [ ] Badlands, USA

- [ ] Bagamoyo, Tanzania
- [ ] Bagan, Myanmar
- [ ] Banaue Rice Terraces, Philippines
- [ ] Band-e Amir, Afghanistan
- [ ] Bandiagara Plateau, Mali
- [ ] Banff National Park, Canada
- [ ] Barbuda, Leeward Islands
- [ ] Barcelona, Spain
- [ ] Barra Grande, Brazil
- [ ] Bath, UK
- [ ] Bauhaus, Germany
- [ ] Bay of Fires, Australia
- [ ] Bay of Fundy, Canada
- [ ] Bay of Islands, New Zealand
- [ ] Belle-Ile-en-Mer, France
- [ ] Berchtesgaden National Park, Germany
- [ ] Berlin, Germany
- [ ] Bern, Switzerland
- [ ] Bialowieza National Park, Poland
- [ ] Big Sur, USA
- [ ] Bitlis, Turkey
- [ ] Black Forest, Germany
- [ ] Bled, Slovenia
- [ ] Blenheim, New Zealand
- [ ] Blue Cave, Croatia
- [ ] Blue Lagoon, Jamaica
- [ ] Blue Mosque, Turkey
- [ ] Blue Mountains, Australia
- [ ] Blyde River Canyon, South Africa
- [ ] Bologna, Italy
- [ ] Borobudur Temple, Indonesia
- [ ] Bremen Market Place, Germany

501 MUST-VISIT DESTINATIONS CHECKLIST

- [ ] British Museum, UK
- [ ] Bruges, Belgium
- [ ] Budapest, Hungary
- [ ] Bukit Lawang, Indonesia
- [ ] Búzios, Brazil
- [ ] Byron Bay, Australia
- [ ] Calgary Stampede, Canada
- [ ] Camargue, France
- [ ] Cape Cross Seal Reserve, Namibia
- [ ] Cape Point, South Africa
- [ ] Cappadocia, Turkey
- [ ] Capri, Italy
- [ ] Carmel-by-the-Sea, USA
- [ ] Carriacou, Granada
- [ ] Caserta, royal palace at, Italy
- [ ] Castel Del Monte, Italy
- [ ] Cat Island, Bahamas
- [ ] Cesky Krumlov, Czech Republic
- [ ] Chao Phraya River, Thailand
- [ ] Charleston, USA
- [ ] Chartres Cathedral, France
- [ ] Chatuchak Market, Thailand
- [ ] Chefchaouen, Morocco
- [ ] Chesil Beach, UK
- [ ] Churchill, Canada
- [ ] Coimbria, Portugal
- [ ] Cologne Cathedral, Germany
- [ ] Córdoba, Spain
- [ ] Coro, Venezuela
- [ ] Cotswolds, UK
- [ ] Cradle Mountain, Australia
- [ ] Custer State Park, South Dakota, USA

- [ ] Cyrene, Libya
- [ ] **D**akhla lagoon, Western Sahara
- [ ] Damascus, Syria
- [ ] Dambulla cave temples, Sri Lanka
- [ ] Dead Sea, Israel
- [ ] Delphi, Greece
- [ ] m Dingle Peninsular, Ireland
- [ ] Divrigi, Turkey
- [ ] Djemila, Algeria
- [ ] Djenne, Mali
- [ ] Dougga, Tunisia
- [ ] Drakensberg Mountains, South Africa
- [ ] Dublin's pubs
- [ ] Dubrovnik, Croatia
- [ ] Durham Castle and Cathedral, UK
- [ ] Dylan Thomas's boathouse, UK
- [ ] **E**aster Island, Chile
- [ ] Edinburgh Castle, UK
- [ ] El Djem, Tunisia
- [ ] El Golea, Algeria
- [ ] Ely Cathedral, UK
- [ ] Ephesus, Turkey
- [ ] Escorial, Spain
- [ ] Étretat, France
- [ ] Évora, Portugal
- [ ] **F**allingwater, USA
- [ ] Fernando de Noronha, Brazil
- [ ] Fès, Morocco
- [ ] Finnish Archipelago (from Helsinki to Turku)
- [ ] Florence, Italy
- [ ] Florianopolis, Brazil 116
- [ ] Florida Everglades, USA

501 MUST-VISIT DESTINATIONS CHECKLIST

- [ ] Florida Keys, USA
- [ ] Fontainebleau, France
- [ ] Galápagos Islands, Ecuador
- [ ] Galle, Sri Lanka
- [ ] Gap of Dunloe, Ireland
- [ ] Gaspe Peninsular, Canada
- [ ] Gda*f*sk, Poland
- [ ] Geneva, Switzerland
- [ ] Giant Redwoods, USA
- [ ] Giant's Causeway, UK 394
- [ ] Giza Pyramids, Egypt
- [ ] God's Pocket, Canada
- [ ] Gondar, Ethiopia
- [ ] Gorée, Isle of, Senegal
- [ ] Gorges de Verdon, France
- [ ] Gorges due Tarn, France
- [ ] Grand Bazaar, Turkey
- [ ] Grand Canyon, USA
- [ ] Grand Erg Occidental Desert, Algeria
- [ ] Grand Palace, Bangkok, Thailand
- [ ] Graz, Austria
- [ ] Great Barrier Reef, Australia
- [ ] Great Lakes, Canada
- [ ] Great Masurian Lakes, Poland
- [ ] Great Ocean Road, Victoria, Australia
- [ ] Great Wall, China
- [ ] Great Zimbabwe Ruins, Zimbabwe
- [ ] Grunwald, Poland
- [ ] Gubbio, Italy
- [ ] Guggenheim Museum, Spain
- [ ] Guilin, China
- [ ] Gwalior, India

- [ ] **H**adrian's Villa, Italy
- [ ] Hagia Sophia, Turkey
- [ ] Hakone, Japan
- [ ] Hateruma Island, Japan
- [ ] Havana, Cuba
- [ ] Herculaneum, Italy
- [ ] Himachal Pradesh, India
- [ ] Himeji, Japan
- [ ] Hoggar, Algeria
- [ ] Hoi An, Vietnam
- [ ] Hollywood, USA
- [ ] Hong Kong, China
- [ ] Horus, Temple of, Egypt
- [ ] Houses of Parliament, UK
- [ ] Huang Long Valley, China
- [ ] Hue, Vietnam
- [ ] Hvar Island, Croatia
- [ ] **I**guazú Falls, Argentina
- [ ] Ilha Grande, Brazil
- [ ] Imperial Palaces of Beijing, China
- [ ] Ironbridge Gorge, UK
- [ ] Isejingu, Shima Hanto, Japan
- [ ] Isfahan, Iran
- [ ] Ivanovo, rock-hewn churches of, Bulgaria
- [ ] Izumo Taisha, Japan
- [ ] **J**ain Temples, India
- [ ] Jaisalmer, India
- [ ] Jerba Island, Tunisia
- [ ] Jericoacoara, Brazil
- [ ] Jerusalem, Israel
- [ ] Juffureh, Gambia
- [ ] Jungfrau mountain, Switzerland

501 MUST-VISIT DESTINATIONS CHECKLIST

- [ ] **K**ailasa, Tibet
- [ ] Kairouan, Tunisia
- [ ] Kakadu National Park, Australia
- [ ] Kanazawa, Japan
- [ ] Kandy, Sri Lanka
- [ ] Karapinar Crater Lakes, Turkey
- [ ] Karen Blixen Museum, Denmark
- [ ] Kauai, USA
- [ ] Kekova, Turkey
- [ ] Kelimutu, Indonesia
- [ ] Ketrzyn, Poland
- [ ] Keukenhof Gardens, Netherlands
- [ ] Kiev Pechersk Lavra, Ukraine
- [ ] Killary Harbour, Ireland
- [ ] Kochi, India
- [ ] Komodo National Park, Indonesia
- [ ] Korcula Island, Croatia
- [ ] Kotor, Montenegro
- [ ] Krak des Chevaliers, Syria
- [ ] Kraków, Poland
- [ ] Kremlin, Russia
- [ ] Kyoto, Japan
- [ ] **L**a Scala, Italy
- [ ] Lake Arenal, Costa Rica
- [ ] Lake Baikal, Russia
- [ ] Lake District, UK
- [ ] Lake Maggiore, Italy–Switzerland
- [ ] Lake Malawi, Malawi
- [ ] Lake Manyara, Tanzania
- [ ] Lake Nakuru National Park, Kenya
- [ ] Lake Pichola, India
- [ ] Lake Tahoe, USA

- [ ] Lake Toba, Indonesia
- [ ] Lake Trasimeno, Italy
- [ ] Lake Turkana, Kenya
- [ ] Lalibela, Ethiopia
- [ ] Lamu Island, Kenya
- [ ] Las Vegas, USA
- [ ] Laurentians, Canada
- [ ] Lavenham, UK
- [ ] Leaning Tower of Pisa, Italy
- [ ] Leptis Magna, Libya
- [ ] Les Calanques, France
- [ ] Levoãa, Slovakia
- [ ] Lhasa, Tibet
- [ ] Lisbon, Portugal
- [ ] Livingstonia, Malawi
- [ ] Lixus, Morocco
- [ ] Lofoten Islands, Norway
- [ ] Loire Valley, France
- [ ] Los Cabos, Mexico
- [ ] Los Jameos del Agua, Spain
- [ ] Louvre, France
- [ ] Luang Prabang, Laos
- [ ] Luangwa, Zambia
- [ ] Lübeck, Germany
- [ ] Lumbini, Nepal
- [ ] Lushan National Park, China
- [ ] **M**achu Picchu, Peru
- [ ] Makalu, Nepal–Tibet border
- [ ] Manado Bay, Indonesia
- [ ] Mandalay, Myanmar
- [ ] Marienburg Castle, Poland
- [ ] Marquesa Islands, French Polynesia

501 MUST-VISIT DESTINATIONS CHECKLIST

- [ ] Marrakesh, Morocco
- [ ] Marseille, France
- [ ] Masai Mara Game Reserve, Kenya
- [ ] Matmata, Tunisia
- [ ] Matobo National Park, Zimbabwe
- [ ] Matsumoto, Japan
- [ ] Mekong Delta, Vietnam
- [ ] Mercantour National Park, France
- [ ] Mesa Verde, USA
- [ ] Miami South Beach, USA
- [ ] Milford Sound, New Zealand
- [ ] Mir Castle, Belarus
- [ ] Mogao Caves, China
- [ ] Monasteries of Popocatepetl, Mexico
- [ ] Monet's Garden at Giverny, France
- [ ] Monte Verde, Brazil
- [ ] Montreal, Canada
- [ ] Montserrat National Park, Spain
- [ ] Mont-St-Michel, France
- [ ] Monument Valley USA
- [ ] Mornington Peninsular, Australia
- [ ] Moscow Metro, Russia
- [ ] Mount Ararat
- [ ] Mount Athos, Greece
- [ ] Mount Bromo, Indonesia
- [ ] Mount Elgon National Park, Kenya
- [ ] Mount Etna, Italy
- [ ] Mount Fuji, Japan
- [ ] Mount Kenya, Kenya
- [ ] Mount Kilimanjaro, Tanzania
- [ ] Mount Olympus, Greece
- [ ] Mount Rushmore, South Dakota, USA

- [ ] Mount Sinai, Egypt
- [ ] Mount St Helens, USA
- [ ] Mozambique, Island of
- [ ] Murchison Falls, Uganda
- [ ] Museum of Modern Art, New York City, USA
- [ ] **N**amib Desert, Namibia
- [ ] National Air and Space Museum, Washington, DC, USA
- [ ] Nemrut Dag, Turkey
- [ ] Neuschwanstein, Germany
- [ ] New England, autumn colours of, USA
- [ ] Ngorongoro Conservation Area, Tanzania
- [ ] Niagara Falls, Canada
- [ ] Niger Delta, Mali
- [ ] Nikko, Japan
- [ ] Niort, France
- [ ] Noosa, Australia
- [ ] Noto, Italy
- [ ] Notre Dame Cathedral, France
- [ ] **O**axaca, Mexico
- [ ] Ogasawara Islands, Japan
- [ ] Ohrid, Macedonia
- [ ] Okanagan Valley, Canada
- [ ] Okavango Delta, Botswana
- [ ] Oktoberfest, Germany
- [ ] Old Man of Hoy, UK
- [ ] Old Town Lijiang and Dali, China
- [ ] Olduvai Gorge, Tanzania
- [ ] Oporto, Portugal
- [ ] Orange, France
- [ ] Orchha, India
- [ ] Orvieto, Italy
- [ ] Ostia Antica, Italy

501 MUST-VISIT DESTINATIONS CHECKLIST

- [ ] Oxford, UK
- [ ] **P**adua, Italy
- [ ] Paestum, Italy
- [ ] Painted Desert, USA
- [ ] Palawan Island, Philippines
- [ ] Pamplona, Spain
- [ ] Pamukkale, Turkey
- [ ] Panang Hill, Malaysia
- [ ] Pantalica, Italy
- [ ] Patagonia, Argentina
- [ ] Patmos, Greece
- [ ] Pembrokeshire Coast, UK
- [ ] Perito Moreno, Argentina
- [ ] Persepolis, Iran
- [ ] Petra, Jordan
- [ ] Phang-Nga Bay, Thailand
- [ ] Pingyao, China
- [ ] Place des Vosges, France
- [ ] Plain of Jars, Laos
- [ ] Polonnaruwa, Sri Lanka
- [ ] Pompeii, Italy
- [ ] Port Antonio, Jamaica
- [ ] Portmeirion, UK
- [ ] Portofino, Italy
- [ ] Prado museum, Spain
- [ ] Prague, Czech Republic
- [ ] Puerto Angel, Mexico
- [ ] Pyramid of Kukulcán, Mexico
- [ ] **Q**uebec City Winter Carnival, Canada
- [ ] Quebec, Canada
- [ ] Queen Charlotte Islands
- [ ] Queenstown, New Zealand

- [ ] **R**aft Cove, Vancouver Island, Canada
- [ ] Rangiroa, French Polynesia
- [ ] Rebun Island, Japan
- [ ] Reichenau, monastic island of, Germany
- [ ] Rhine Valley, Germany
- [ ] Rift Valley, Kenya
- [ ] Riga, Latvia
- [ ] Rijksmuseum, Netherlands
- [ ] Rio de Janeiro, Brazil
- [ ] rock carvings of Tanum, Sweden
- [ ] Rome, Italy
- [ ] Rotorua, New Zealand
- [ ] Rottnest Island, Australia
- [ ] Rwanda National Park, Rwanda
- [ ] Rwenzori Mountains National Park, Uganda
- [ ] **S**aba, Leeward Islands
- [ ] St Augustine, USA
- [ ] Sainte-Chapelle, France
- [ ] Saint-Louis, Senegal
- [ ] St Petersburg, Russia
- [ ] St Sophia Cathedral, Ukraine
- [ ] St-Tropez, France
- [ ] Salisbury Cathedral, UK
- [ ] Saltaire, UK
- [ ] Salvador, Brazil
- [ ] Salzburg, Austria
- [ ] Samaria Gorge, Greece
- [ ] Samarkand, Uzbekistan
- [ ] San Antonia, USA
- [ ] San Augustín Archaeological Park, Colombia
- [ ] San Diego, USA
- [ ] San Francisco, USA

501 MUST-VISIT DESTINATIONS CHECKLIST

- [ ] San Gimignano, Italy
- [ ] Sana'a, Yemen
- [ ] Santa Cruz Carnival, Bolivia
- [ ] Santa Fe, USA
- [ ] Santa María de Guadalupe, Spain
- [ ] Santiago de Compostela, Spain
- [ ] Santorini, Greece
- [ ] Sausalito, USA
- [ ] Savannah, USA
- [ ] Schwedagon Pawa, Myanmar
- [ ] Scottish Highlands, UK
- [ ] Scottish Lochs, UK
- [ ] Sedona, USA
- [ ] Serengeti National Park, Tanzania
- [ ] Shanghai, China
- [ ] Shimanami Kaido, Japan
- [ ] Shiretoko National Park, Japan
- [ ] Sidi Ifni, Morocco
- [ ] Siena, Italy
- [ ] Sighisoara, Romania
- [ ] Sigiriya Fortress, Sri Lanka
- [ ] Silhouette Island, Seychelles
- [ ] Simien National Park, Ethiopia
- [ ] Sinharaja Forest Reserve, Sri Lanka
- [ ] Sintra, Portugal
- [ ] Siwa Oasis, Egypt
- [ ] Skeleton Coast, Namibia
- [ ] Skopje, Macedonia
- [ ] Smoky Mountains, USA
- [ ] Snowdon and Snowdonia, UK
- [ ] Socotra, Yemen
- [ ] Sozopol, Bulgaria

- [ ] Spanish Riding School, Austria
- [ ] Spirits Bay, New Zealand
- [ ] Spitzkoppe, Namibia
- [ ] Split, Croatia
- [ ] Srinagar, India
- [ ] Statue of Liberty, USA
- [ ] Stockholm, Sweden
- [ ] Stonehenge, UK
- [ ] Stratford-upon-Avon, UK
- [ ] Sudd, Sudan
- [ ] Suffolk Heritage Coast, UK
- [ ] Sumela Monastery, Turkey
- [ ] Sydney Harbour, Australia
- [ ] Symi, Greece
- [ ] **T**able Mountain, South Africa
- [ ] Tad Lo Falls, Laos
- [ ] Tafraoute, Morocco
- [ ] Taj Mahal, India
- [ ] Tallinn, Estonia
- [ ] Taman Negara National Park, Malaysia
- [ ] Tangier, Morocco
- [ ] Taormina, Italy
- [ ] Taos, USA
- [ ] Taroudant, Morocco
- [ ] Tassili N'Ajjer, Algeria
- [ ] Tate Modern, UK
- [ ] Tay Ninh, Vietnam
- [ ] Tayrona National Park, Columbia
- [ ] Temple of Edfu, Egypt
- [ ] Temple of Karnak, Luxor, Egypt
- [ ] Temple of Poseidon, Greece
- [ ] Teotihuacán, Mexico

501 MUST-VISIT DESTINATIONS CHECKLIST

- [ ] Tintern Abbey, UK
- [ ] Tioman Island, Malaysia
- [ ] Tivoli Gardens, Denmark
- [ ] Tokaj wine region, Hungary
- [ ] Topkapi Palace, Turkey
- [ ] Torre Annunziata, Italy
- [ ] Toulouse-Lautrec Museum
- [ ] Tower of London, UK
- [ ] Trancoso, Brazil
- [ ] Tresco, UK
- [ ] Troy, Turkey
- [ ] Tsavo National Park, Kenya
- [ ] Tunis, Tunisia
- [ ] Tunnels of Cu Chi, Vietnam
- [ ] **U**bud, Indonesia
- [ ] Uluru (Ayers Rock), Australia
- [ ] Urbino, Italy
- [ ] Urnes Stave Church
- [ ] **V**alletta, Malta
- [ ] Valley of the Kings, Luxor, Egypt
- [ ] Van Gogh Museum, Netherlands
- [ ] Vancouver, Canada
- [ ] Vancouver Island, Canada
- [ ] Varanasi, India
- [ ] Vatican City, Rome
- [ ] Venice, Italy
- [ ] Victoria Falls, Zambia–Zimbabwe border
- [ ] Vienna, Austria
- [ ] Vientiane, Laos
- [ ] Vietnam Veterans' Memorial, Washington, DC, USA
- [ ] Volubilis, Morocco
- [ ] **W**ashington, DC, USA

- [ ] Wat Phou, Laos
- [ ] Wat Tham Pha, Thailand
- [ ] Wengen, Switzerland
- [ ] West Norwegian fjords, Norway
- [ ] Whistler Mountain, Canada
- [ ] White Desert, Egypt
- [ ] Whitsunday Islands, Australia
- [ ] Wieliczka Salt Mine, Poland
- [ ] Wineglass Bay, Australia
- [ ] Wolong Nature Reserve, China
- [ ] Wounded Knee, USA
- [ ] **Y**aku Island, Japan
- [ ] Yarra Valley, Australia
- [ ] Yellowstone National Park, USA
- [ ] Yogyakarta, Indonesia
- [ ] Yorkshire Dales, UK
- [ ] Yosemite National Park, USA
- [ ] **Z**agreb, Croatia
- [ ] Zakopane, Poland
- [ ] Zanzibar, Tanzania
- [ ] Zomba, Malawi
- [ ] Zuma Market, Madagascar

First published in 2009 by Bounty Books,
a division of Octopus Publishing Group Ltd
2–4 Heron Quays, London E14 4JP
www.octopusbooks.co.uk

An Hachette UK Company
www.hachette.co.uk

Copyright © Octopus Publishing Group Ltd 2009

All rights reserved. No part of this work may be reproduced or utilized in
any form or by any means, electronic or mechanical, including photocopying,
recording or by any information storage and retrieval system, without the
prior written permission of the publisher

ISBN: 978-0-753716-98-4

A CIP catalogue record for this book is available from the British Library

Printed and bound in China

Cover Photography: Corbis/Brian A. Vikander

Inside Photography:

Alamy/Tristan Deschamps 153; /Barry Mason 97

Corbis/David Ball 213; /Brakefield Photo/Brand X 61; /B.S.P.I. 73; /Tony Craddock/zefa 209; /Werner
Forman 37, 45; /Free Agents Limited 125; /Walter Geiersperger 69; /Wolfgang Kaehler 145; /Bob Krist
57; /Frans Lemmens/zefa 133; /Barry Lewis 205; /Ludovic Maisant 89; /Gunter Marx Photography 113;
/Gideon Mendel 105; /David Samuel Robbins 101; /Galen Rowell 201; /Louie Psihoyos 53; /Jose Fuste
Raga 219; /Brian A. Vikander 77; /Ronald W. Weir/zefa 85; /Larry Williams 93; /Michael S. Yamashita 2

Cartography 8-13 © Philip's